Happy seventieth!
Love— Mary

BEING SEVENTY

BEING SEVENTY

SEVENTY

The Measure of a Year

Elizabeth Gray Vining

The Viking Press, New York

First published in 1978 by The Viking Press
625 Madison Avenue, New York, N.Y. 10022
Published simultaneously in Canada by
Penguin Books Canada Limited
Printed in U.S.A.
2 3 4 5 82 81 80 79 78

Library of Congress Cataloging in Publication Data
Vining, Elizabeth Gray, Being Seventy.
1. Vining, Elizabeth Gray—Diaries.
2. Authors, American—20th century—Biography. I. Title.
PS3572.I55Z464 813'.5'2 77-25480
ISBN 0-670-15539-x

ACKNOWLEDGEMENT
"A Reflection" is from *Selected Poems of Robert Nathan*.
Copyright 1935 and renewed 1963 by Robert Nathan. Reprinted
by permission of Alfred A. Knopf, Inc.

BEING SEVENTY

Four Seasons fill the measure of the Year;
There are four seasons in the mind of man.

John Keats

Saturday, August 26, 1972

I wish I could stop thinking about being old. It's not that I mind it so much or fear it; it's just that I am so aware of it all the time. I catch sight of myself in a mirror and think, "My God, is that what I look like now? But then I am nearly seventy. Of course I look like that." My elbow stabs me and I think, "Arthritis. About time for it." Or I stumble on the stairs and think, "Old and clumsy. I suppose I'll get worse." A name or a word eludes my mind, and I think, "Losing my memory. That is probably the *worst*." I am enjoying a luncheon party with lively conversation and laughter, and suddenly the thought comes, "Four widows over sixty-five having a good time as if they were young. How absurd."

It isn't as if I felt old. I don't. Inside I feel often as gauche, as shy, as incapable of wise or effective action as I did at sixteen, or as surprised and delighted by unexpected beauty. But in actual fact I shall be seventy on my birthday, which occurs in a little more than a month.

Not that seventy today is what it used to be. Modern medicinal science, from antibiotics to contact lenses; modern food, from pasteurized milk to frozen lobster tails; sensible clothes, comfortable houses, a refreshing variety of activities, interests, and opportunities have kept us mentally vigorous and physically healthy, so that eighty is what seventy used to be and seventy is more like sixty. Even so, in the buried currents of thought, seventy represents a finality.

Though I am not an assiduous reader of the Bible, its wisdom and its cadences are bred in my bones and deep in the fibers of my mind. "The days of our years are threescore years and ten; and if by reason of strength they be fourscore years, yet is their strength labour and sorrow; for it is soon cut off, and we fly away." I can write the words without hesitation, but I must look in the Concordance to see where they come from. (Psalm 90, that wonderful one, which begins, "Lord, thou hast been our dwelling place in all generations," and ends, "And let the beauty of the Lord our God be upon us: and establish thou the work of our hands upon us; yea, the work of our hands establish thou it.") Even optimistic Emerson wrote, "I reckon my seventieth birthday as the close of youth."

A door shuts. It is shut not in one's face but behind

one. In front is a new landscape, bleak perhaps at times, lit no doubt at others with mysterious beauty, but cut off in the distance by a wall, which for the first time is close enough to be visible. One stands in a limited space, with the door behind and the wall somewhere in front.

In younger years one said lightly, "I don't want to live forever. I certainly don't want to grow old the way Aunt Hester has." And one quoted cheerily the Gaelic proverb, "Save when he comes too late, death is a friend."

A friend he is, I truly believe, but a formidable one; a friend to be anticipated and prepared for as well as welcomed. And his harbingers—those officials who in Elizabethan days and earlier preceded the royal personage, conferring with the prospective host, preparing rooms, making demands—his harbingers are often weariness, illness, pain, and mental diminishment. We may, of course, meet him unexpectedly in the earlier years, but after seventy we are certain to encounter him soon, and his shadow often walks beside us in the new landscape.

Being seventy is not a matter of a single day. It takes a year; it is not finished till one is seventy-one. And so I think I shall pay special attention to this new year as it turns, keep a journal of its changes and its insights, of the things I do or think for the first time because I am the age I am, and of those things I do for the last time or enjoy less keenly, of the compensations as well as the diminishments, and of the unexpected delights, for I am sure that there will be flowers in this landscape that do not grow elsewhere, and glimpses of unforeseen heights.

Rain. I hear it dropping and splashing outside. A wet wind stirs and brings the roar of Philadelphia in rising and falling swirls. I am seventy today.

My best birthday present is that Tané and Yukio Matsumura are with me on their way home from a trip to Europe. Tané Takahashi, the interpreter and secretary and beloved "little sister" of the four years I spent in Japan teaching the Crown Prince, married Yukio Matsumura a little less than a year ago. In fact, all three of the Takahashi sisters, all spinsters in their fifties, have married within the past year, which must be some kind of record. Yukio, too, I have known for many years, ever since 1947, when, as a young husband and father of a seven-month-old baby, he used to walk several miles each morning in the dawn to get milk from a farm. His first wife, Matsue, died two years ago. We are all going to the Rubels' for dinner tonight, but the Rubels, though they are old friends, don't know that it is a birthday party.

Birthdays have never been a big feature of my life, except during the years when Morgan was with me. A month after we first met in Chapel Hill, he celebrated my twenty-fourth birthday by taking me to the Carolina Inn for dinner, and all the birthdays after that were lit with glory, until my thirty-first, when I lay flat on my back in the hospital without him.

I remember running away from my third birthday party, and the family forgot my twenty-first altogether. As

6

I grew older, friends gave beautiful parties for me, usually dinner parties, warm and gay. When I was in Japan the Imperial Family always sent me flowers (once eight different kinds of orchids in one bouquet) and exquisite presents, but I cannot remember any of my childhood birthdays at all between the third and the twenty-first, except, oddly, one.

I was eight, I think. I was playing with my friend Elizabeth Hutchinson, and we went in to see her grandparents, who lived next door in a large stone house. They both seemed to me incredibly old, he with his white beard and she with her black silk dress. I suppose, actually, they were no older in 1910 than I am now. When it was made known—I forget whether by Elizabeth or by me—that this was my birthday, Mrs. Shillingford said, "We must do something about that." She bustled away and came back with a package all tied up in white tissue paper and pink ribbon. Inside was a small sweet-grass basket.

She probably forgot next day that she had done it, and I doubt that I gave her any idea of the surprise and delight I felt, but today, after sixty-odd years, the memory of that little basket and the grace of the gift are still fragrant in my mind.

Later. Among the cards and presents today was a birthday letter from a fan, who got the date out of *Quiet Pilgrimage,* my autobiography, which carried me to age sixty, and which she said she enjoyed reading. After some conventional good wishes she regaled me with an account of an acquaintance of hers in Canada, who was not seen for several days. A search was made, but all they found were three of her fingers in the garbage pail. I suppose this bizarre horror was on her mind and so got into a birthday letter to a stranger. Canada has seemed to me saner and quieter than the United States, but evidently shocking things happen there too.

Saturday, October 7

Dashing into the Acme to get a half-pint of cream, I saw two young men, Americans, gotten up in an extraordinary way. They wore white Indian-like robes; their heads were shaved except for long tails of limp hair falling from their crowns to their shoulder blades. Two white lines were painted on their foreheads and down each side of their noses. They were doing a quite unexotic kind of marketing—packages of breakfast foods, cans of fruit juice, and the like. As I stood in the express line with my own small carton, waiting, one of them with his cart full of items charged up to me and said, "Can I go in front of you?"

I said, "Why?"—which frightened him so that he rushed away, without answering, to another line.

I really wondered why. Because he was in a hurry? But then so was I, and I had only one package. Because he was a holy man? I would have loved to hear him say so. But he only ran off.

Thursday, October 12

Clara Sipprell and Phyllis Fenner take pleasure in grave-

8

yards. They enjoy walking in beautiful ones and looking at the stones, which they consider a record rather than a pious tribute. The cemetery in Manchester, Vermont, is a particularly lovely and peaceful one, and some time ago they bought a plot there. They have a good deal of fun planning what they will do with it.

Yesterday morning at breakfast in their butternut-paneled kitchen, looking over the frosted garden (overnight temperature 20 degrees), they told me of their plans for the plot. Some time ago at the Art Center on the edge of Manchester they spotted the stone they wanted, a large shale rock embedded in the field, and bought it. Recently they found a man who for one hundred dollars would dig up the rock and transport it to the cemetery. The next stage will be designing and ordering a bronze plaque to be placed on it. To their own names and dates will be added that of Clara's much-loved and honored friend and mentor whose ashes were many years ago scattered to the winds. Her name and dates will be there "for the record." At the top will be a quotation (from whom I have forgotten, and also the exact words), saying something like: "To the gentle influences of nature we commend our dead."

There has been much joking about this at the Art Center, they tell me serenely. It seems to me a fresh and admirable handling of a problem often approached morbidly or perfunctorily or callously. At one extreme is the Japanese cult of graveyard respect and ceremony, the prescribed visits on certain days taking precedence over all other duties and pleasures. At the other is our modern shudder-

9

ing away from the whole subject and the casual scattering of ashes in gardens.

Graveyards attached to churches or meetinghouses—like the beautiful one at the Church of the Redeemer in Bryn Mawr, Pennsylvania, complete with medieval lych-gate, or the old one at Germantown Meeting in Philadelphia, where uniform low white stones march decorously under great trees—have a traditional and a religious aura that I like. But commercial cemeteries, from the fashionable Laurel Hill above the Schuylkill to the garish Holy Sepulchre outside the city, have always set my teeth on edge. Our own plot is at Ivy Hill, a small, unfashionable, but relatively inoffensive cemetery; it is at the edge of the graveyard, under a big tree, and our graves are marked by low stones similar to the Quaker ones, as my Episcopalian father directed. My parents' graves are in the first row, and in the second are Morgan's and Violet's, with a space for mine between. It is nearly three years since my beloved sister died. When she was seventy, I was only fifty-one. I remember distinctly that she said she enjoyed being seventy, and she enjoyed, I believe, all the years of that decade. It was not until she got into the eighties that strokes overtook her.

I go to Ivy Hill only if I cannot avoid it, at the time of funerals or periodically to see that the perpetual care is maintained as it should be. I think that Clara and Phyllis have a more civilized as well as a more interesting attitude. The day before yesterday, Tuesday, I drove the Matsumuras to Manchester. The day was utterly beautiful, October at its sparkling best. We started a little after nine and got there at five-thirty, covering about four hundred miles of lovely country—the edge of the Poconos, the edge of the Catskills, the edge of the Berkshires, ending up at the foot of Mount Equinox—the autumn coloring at its height the whole way. Yukio was ecstatic. He said it was worth coming all the way to America just for that ride alone; he marveled at the size of the United States and the great breadth of its vistas.

Manchester itself was beautiful, with its wide village street, tall elms, stately white houses. Clara and Phyllis had arranged for the Matsumuras to stay at the inn across the street, while I slept in Phyllis's study. We had dinner at their eighteenth-century French oak table, with candles in silver candlesticks, and a fire on the hearth, surrounded by treasures from Japan, Yugoslavia, Italy, Switzerland. Over the mantel hangs a flight of copper birds by an American artist.

The next morning, yesterday, as beautiful a day but with mistier distances, I kissed Tané good-by and drove home. Their visit to me was, I think, a success. Certainly I enjoyed it. It was a strenuous week, with a great deal of driving—about a thousand miles in all—and meal planning and preparing as well, though I was greatly helped by the friends who invited us out and by Yukio's grand dinner party on the revolving top floor of the Holiday Inn, from which we could see the lights of Philadelphia spread

11

out between its rivers. I am tired now, but not too tired, and elated because I could do it. My years do not burden me.

The drive home alone was pleasant, with all the same beauty seen from another angle and under a different sort of light. I found stacks of mail waiting but nothing very interesting except a letter from the Ossabaw Island Residential Foundation saying that I may spend four or five weeks there from the middle of February. This is a writers' colony, different, so I am told, from all the others. It will be a new and interesting venture, and I should get a lot of writing done.

Today I am resting and catching up, for tonight I must make that speech to the New Century Guild. I promised to do it months ago, when I had no idea at all that Tané and Yukio would be coming. That is the trouble with speech commitments. They nearly always turn out to be highly inconvenient when the time comes.

Saturday, October 14

Walking along Germantown Avenue in Chestnut Hill this morning, I passed two women talking. They were pleasantly dressed, not young, not notable in any way. After I had passed, I heard one say, "Well, *I* don't want to live that long. I don't have anyone to take care of *me*."

There was something universal in her cry. A whole generation of women, weary of caring for, in present-day difficulties and high costs, their parents, aunts, older sisters, looks with bleak eyes at their own prospects. Even those with devoted daughters do not feel the old assurance that it is right and inevitable that they should be cared for by their children to the end. The burden has become too heavy. It goes on too long.

In the afternoon Eliza Foulke, an eighty-two-year-old friend happily tucked away in the Quaker retirement center, Foulkeways, told me that what old people want is security, privacy, and independence—and independence not least of the three. By independence she meant "not being told what to do." Surely love is needed too. But Eliza gives so much love that she would not think to mention it.

Sunday, October 15

Most of yesterday, from nine-fifteen to three-thirty, I spent at the Haverford Corporation meeting, the annual meeting of the powerless body that makes the doings of the Haverford College Board of Managers legal. They have turned a legal formality into an opportunity to give more than a hundred people a sympathetic picture of the college. There is also a good meal and much meeting of friends and acquaintances—a party, in fact.

This year they have added some thirty-five women. When I first went on the Corporation, Mary Hoxie Jones, Charlotte Read, and I were the only women. Last year we were asked to recommend others. The three I suggested were there today—and one of them kindly and somewhat condescendingly welcomed me to the gathering.

The campus looked beautiful in the October sunshine. When a simple Pennsylvania farm was turned into a campus a hundred and thirty-odd years ago, the Quaker planners sent to England for a landscape gardener, who planted it with quincunxes of trees—a beech, an oak, a chestnut, a maple, a pine—and a few of the original trees still stand majestically in the lovely patterns of the first planting. Founders Hall, plain and dignified with wide porches, still commands the center of the campus. We met in Stokes Hall, where there is a small auditorium with all the modern amenities.

Several of the best and most "relevant" statements in the day's reports turned out to be quotations from Rufus Jones and Isaac Sharpless, giants of the past. A black student, a sophomore, reported for the student body. In this period of student sloppiness he was refreshingly well-dressed and well-groomed; his voice was rich and his diction without local voice accent of any kind, Southern or Philadelphian. In the present freshman class of two hundred and fifty students only six—in spite of valiant efforts on the part of the administration and the board—are black. I contribute annually to the United Negro College Fund. It may be that in the present transitional stage the upgrading of the Negro colleges will be more useful than the competition among traditionally white colleges for able black students.

Having read a good many issues of the *Bryn Mawr–Haverford News* during the past year, I knew that all was not quite as smooth and orderly as it was presented to us, although the President spoke frankly of failures and losses. Required Collection—a quaint Quaker term for Assembly—is gone, as is required meeting for worship. He

14

regrets that. Freshman English was taken off three or four years ago but put back this year. I don't suppose that meeting for worship will ever be required again. The Quaker meeting is peculiarly vulnerable. An Episcopal service can drown out mutters with organ music, hymns, and psalms, but you cannot force rebellious young men to worship in silence.

Gerhard Spiegler, formerly professor of religion, now Provost, a much loved and respected man, spoke of the academic side of Haverford. He is just back from a year's study in Europe, and he reported that the European universities are far more directed toward professions and less concerned with liberal arts than American ones. Speaking of Haverford's Quaker basis, he said it was a *caring* place, where religion issued in daily acts. This is high praise.

Wednesday, October 18

This morning after breakfast I walked all around the apartment house grounds, past the other buildings and along the edge of the Wissahickon woods, all around the field, along the driveway through the woods to School Lane, across the lawn under the big trees, some of which, the linden and the copper beech, are on the list of seventy Registered Trees of Philadelphia, past the ginkgo, tall and golden, and the old cherry to the side door into the A-Building. I can do it in half an hour or less, but lingering as I did, I took nearly an hour. The sky was a pale blue with a thin curdle of clouds, the sun pale gold; the air was nippy. In the field the tall grasses were rosy and the sumac at the edges was red, but there was still a background of dark green in the woods. The trees and bushes were full of small birds: chickadees, titmice, juncos, kinglets, warblers, all moving from branch to ground, from ground to branch, and from branch to branch, keeping up a bright cheeping and chirping.

How often have I taken this walk in the five years that I have lived here? Three or four times a week. Almost always there has been something special to tuck away in my memory: a cock pheasant strutting through the grass, a chipmunk sitting in the center of a hole into an old stump, just like an illustration in a children's book, a Canada warbler with his black necklace on his white vest. And all the time the noise of cars rushing along Wissahickon Drive down below.

Thursday, October 19

Snow! For three hours or so the air was full of large, wet flakes, which melted on the streets but lay like a veil over grass and accumulated on roofs. Later it turned to rain, the sky darkened, the wind was wet and penetratingly cold. It was peculiarly dreary.

Monday, October 23

Judy Rubel and I drove across the Delaware into New Jersey to Brigantine Wildlife Sanctuary. I love to go there, either in a serious ornithological mood with a group and a knowledgeable leader, spilling out of cars to peer through a telescope at distant birds, checking a list at the end of the day, or more relaxedly with one companion to drift slowly along the dikes, enjoying whatever we see easily and eating lunch in the car at some casual spot. Judy was delightful, a good talker and a good listener, knowing birds I did not, sometimes not knowing the birds I did.

It was a changeable October day, occasionally overcast, but with the glare and glisten dimmed a little it was easier to see the birds' colors and markings. We did not have many to put on a list, but we came to know a few a little better. And such color! Blue of sky and deeper blue of water, gold or russet of marsh grass, brilliant white of egrets and of swans. Great blue heron stood in the reeds or suddenly beside the road lifted themselves slowly into the air. White-rumped marsh hawks, a pair of them, wheeled in a dance together in the sky. Coots were busy in chummy groups. Three pied-billed grebes, swimming sedately, inspired Judy to say, "They look like bathtub animals, don't they?" and suddenly I saw her as a young mother bending over a pair of cherubs in a bathtub. There were Canada geese in great numbers, a few brant, and some dramatically beautiful snow geese. Perhaps the climax was a peregrine falcon with his small, flat head and dark markings, his wide, pointed wings and long, narrow tail, flying over the marsh grass and sailing up to perch in a dead tree near the woods. A bittern with bicolored wings, light and dark, flew out of the reeds beside the dike and then dived back into them and disappeared.

Undoubtedly we missed many. Flocks of sandpipers or semipalmated plovers or whatnot flew and wheeled without our naming them. But we savored what we saw, and drank deep of wild beauty, while off in the distance, beyond the marshes and the water, the hotels of Atlantic City stood in a serrated line against the sky.

Wednesday, October 25

The art teacher at Germantown Friends School asked me two weeks ago to bring samples of Japanese art to her classes, and I lightheartedly agreed. This evening I have been gathering together some portable pieces: pictures of the Hōryūji wall paintings to represent eighth-century art; Kawai Gyukudō's painting of a pond in autumn, which the Empress Dowager gave me; some prints by Utamaro, Hiroshige, and others, and the modern Kyoshi Saito; the Crown Prince's black lacquer box with the gold phoenix on it, and the Princesses' gold lacquer poem box with their poems inside; an old book on calligraphy, a *tsuzuri bako*, containing inkstone, water box, ink stick, and brushes, and a miniature one without the water box, a Japanese precursor of the fountain pen. I imagine that the students will want to spend a good deal of time on calligraphy. Their teacher says some of them have been trying it themselves.

After some rummaging in closets I found the wooden box that originally contained the dry lacquer replica of the eighth-century Kwannon at Chuguji Temple, which stands in the niche by the fireplace, and carefully put the little statue in it. Then I added to the collection a small but exquisite cloisonné vase that the Empress gave me, and a

18

piece of beautiful handweaving in heavy blue and white homespun cotton kept unseen these many years in a bureau drawer; a brown and cream-colored vase made by the great potter Kawai Kanjirō in his early days, and his book of poems printed on handmade paper in both Japanese and English. I pulled out of the bookcase two of the best Western books on Japanese art, both of them short, interesting, and unpretentious: Langdon Warner's *The Enduring Art of Japan* and Hugo Munsterberg's *The Folk Art of Japan.* It is a mixed collection, and a Westerner might think it contained more crafts than arts, but a Japanese would not make that distinction.

It will be interesting to see what takes hold of the kids' imagination and rouses their enthusiasm, how much they know about Japan to begin with.

Thursday, October 26

The visit to G. F. S. with my treasures went off well. I talked to three high-school classes informally, with an exchange of questions and comments, and the students were completely absorbed and enthusiastic about my things—after they got there. Their teacher told me that she had made an especial appeal to them to be on time, as an act of respect to the visitor, but about half of them sauntered in ten minutes or more late. Apparently at G. F. S. they now come and go at will.

Carrying all the things up to the third floor and then back again to the car was fairly strenuous and took several trips. The art teacher helped me, but no husky student was called upon to assist—or felt an impulse to offer help. It is a great temptation to look back and say, "Things were different in my day," with the implication if not the outright assertion that they were better. And then I think of Whittier in his twenties writing derisively:

> *O dear! O dear! I grieve, I grieve*
> *For the good old days of Adam and Eve.*

Saturday, October 28

To the airport in the rain to meet my Irish friend Helen Campbell's plane at 8:20 p.m. She arrived tired and strained but very glad to be here. We sat up late talking, and she gave me a vivid glimpse of life in Belfast today.

Sunday, October 29

After meeting for worship this morning Helen spoke to a packed Adult Class—about what it is like to live in Northern Ireland now, the complicated and intense emotions and especially the implacable hardness of the extreme Protestants. A Quaker herself, she is against violence of any kind, but it seemed to me that she was a little more tender toward the I. R. A. than toward the "Prots." At least, she had seen a Catholic woman cry over a dead Protestant boy, whereas the extreme Protestants are stony-faced.

A good part of her life—and she is two years older than I—she has spent working for better feeling between the two groups. A pioneer in early childhood education, she

20

has established nursery schools and playgrounds in which small children of both persuasions could play together and their mothers meet. She was one of the founders of the Irish Association, a cultural organization made up of both Protestants and Catholics, and she is a member of the New Ulster Movement and of Women Together. But they all seem to be feeling rather hopeless. Nobody will predict anything encouraging for the future. In a very moving close she asked for our prayers.

Wednesday, November 1. Rain

Today we went to see *Sounder*, a beautifully acted and photographed film about a black sharecropper family in Louisiana in 1933. We entered just as the picture was beginning, and, the theater being dark, we slipped into two empty seats on the next to the last row on the side.

As my eyes became accustomed to the dimness, I realized that the theater was full of schoolchildren, many, if not most of them, black. Some adolescents in the row behind us talked loudly, making jeering remarks about the film. Thinking that they were white and were being offensive to the blacks in the audience, I officiously—and unwisely—said, "Sh!" That opened the floodgates.

From then on through the two hours of the movie, their principal pleasure lay in trying to bait us. Some samples:

"Nobody knows how I hate whites."

"Black is beautiful, yellow is together, white is shit."

"Once they wouldn't have let us come to this theater.

21

This is a movie for black people. We oughtn't to let *them* in."

"Shh!" Very loudly and derisively. "Shh!"

"Don't white people get ugly when they get old?"

"They sure do. Their hair gets such an ugly color."

"Their faces get ugly. They get red and gray."

"Shh. Shh."

"I hate white people."

From time to time they would seize the backs of our seats and shake them violently.

We did not move to other seats. There was a black policeman, pistols at his belt, standing with his arms folded, behind the last row in the middle. He did not stir or turn his head in our direction, but he was there. I had no fear of physical violence, and I was interested to see how long the youngsters would keep this up and whether the appeal of the movie itself would in the end take hold of them. Helen was aware that they were talking at us, but the unfamiliar accent kept her from understanding much that they said. When I told her afterward what I remembered of the remarks, she said that it was much like Ireland, that the British soldiers made similar comments about the Roman Catholics.

After a while, since the adolescents behind us could get no reaction out of us, they turned their attention back to the film, but not in the way that I expected. They and other young blacks in the theater were not moved by it as I was. I heard a good deal of derisive laughter. Only once one of the girls behind me revealed herself and her feeling. When the black man in the film spoke tenderly to his son, she said, "Wish my dad would talk to me that way." Beautiful as the film was visually, and to me heart-twisting, with the scenes in the courthouse and the prison camp and the desperate poverty of the black family, still I realized that it was a sentimental story done from an essentially white point of view. The white woman who was kind to the black children at risk to herself, the tenderness of the black man toward his family, the exemplary behavior of the children: it was all too good. The mother was acted so superbly by the black actress that she was lifted onto another plane altogether, the plane of the authenticity of her art, but I saw the weaknesses of the film in the midst of those young blacks as I would probably not have done in a quiet theater filled with white people.

When the movie was over and the lights went on, the schoolchildren were all herded out through doors at the far end of the theater. Helen and I went out at the back and found a large crowd packed in the lobby, waiting to get in, almost all of them white. They will see a different film from the one we saw, I thought.

Now, writing about it at four a.m., I think of one more thing that I noticed. The crowded theater did not smell of unwashed bodies as once it would have done, whether the children were black or white. These city schoolchildren now have the means to keep clean. Some progress, after all, has been made here and there.

This morning, out on an errand, I ran into a fellow member of Germantown Meeting and we stopped to talk about Meeting affairs. Then we got off on other subjects, and I told her the story I heard the other day about another meeting.

Scene: a staid old meetinghouse, meeting for worship in full depth of silence. Elderly woman gets up and makes sweet little platitudinous talk about the glory of the autumn morning and the glory of God. She has barely sat down when a young man with long hair, a beard, and blue jeans rises, shouts, "Bullshit!" and stalks out, leaving the meeting stunned. My friend said she could well imagine it.

Not long ago she was a member of a committee that was trying to meet the demands of the Black Economic Development Council. In the course of the discussion the son of a "weighty Friend" peppered his opinions with the word "bullshit." When she was asked for her point of view, she said that the language had so disturbed her that she was not able to think clearly on the subject. Whereupon the young Friend went into a rage and stamped out. After that all the rest of the committee turned on *her* and accused her of hypocrisy in objecting to language that everyone knew was commonly used.

It teases the mind to consider which words are offensive and which are not. I have to drive myself, even in the privacy of my study, to type the word "bullshit," yet I can write "cow manure" without a qualm. I could not use either one as an expletive—but then neither could I shout "Nonsense!" at someone with whom I did not agree. Or at least not in a meeting for worship and probably not in a committee meeting.

Perhaps the thing about both incidents that troubles me most is the way that the young seem to have, these days, of announcing explosively their disagreement or disdain and then turning on their heels and walking out. I can think of several other instances of the same kind of response recently on the part of young men. How is anything to be put right if they are not willing to stay and explain and defend their point of view? How can we confused and affronted—but also often ready to compromise and even to be convinced—old people help to reach a resolution of the conflict?

Or do they just want us not to be so tiresome? Did I never walk out myself when I was young? Certainly I can remember wanting to.

Friday, November 3

Helen yesterday said something rather interesting about aging. I wish I could remember it exactly. It was something about recognizing and accepting that one is no longer useful to—or perhaps it was "necessary to"—anyone, but taking strength from the fact that one has been useful in the past. "Yea, the work of our hands establish thou it."

If we can just manage to carry our own weight and not use up the lives of younger people taking care of us! Dear

Peggy, the friend in this apartment house, with whom I used to read every Monday night and whom I sorely miss, had for the last years of her life three middle-aged women doing nothing but just taking care of her. But then, it was a way for them to earn their living, wasn't it?

Monday, November 6

I have my plane ticket to Tokyo for November 14, first class, as a guest of the Japan Center of the P.E.N. Club.* They invited me in the spring to be a "distinguished observer" at their conference, first tentatively, by a telephone call from New York, then formally by a letter and a silk-bound prospectus. I accepted, not without qualms, for it is a great deal to accept, and what can I contribute? But I was tempted beyond my power to resist. I can go, I wrote in my journal, and sit quietly and learn. Moreover, I can stay on longer at my own expense and see my friends.

This conference on Japanese civilization, to which scholars from all over the world will come, seems to me a wise and realistic move on Japan's part now. In view of China's opening up and Nixon's blind insensitiveness toward Japan on one hand, and on the other Japan's own headlong rush into economic growth and prosperity, it is appropriate to draw attention to her ancient culture, her history, her unchanging essence. "We feel the absolute necessity of a cultural interchange and cooperation which

*International Association of Poets, Playwrights, Editors, Essayists and Novelists.

26

would bring about a true understanding between nations of varied cultures—one that cannot be obtained through political means," says the prospectus.

I remember in Honolulu hearing that wonderful old Friend, Cathy Cox, say, "Youth is for learning; middle age is for doing; old age is for enjoying." When you are old—as I to my astonishment now am—learning is also enjoying. One comes full circle in more ways than entering second childhood.

Tuesday, November 7. Sunny

Election Day. Nobody is saying very much about it. In the circles in which I move there are many McGovern buttons, but nobody thinks he has a chance. Nixon manages to make people believe that he is firm and strong and capable, even though again and again he has turned against what he himself proposed—welfare reform, the reduction of arms treaty with Russia, the agreement with Vietnam. The worst bombing of the war came a day or two ago, when negotiations were apparently at a finishing point.

Near me in the line at the polls was a woman with a distinguished old Philadelphia name, talking animatedly with the man standing next to her.

"I have a black fellow working for me. I asked him who he was going to vote for and he said, 'Well, I can't vote for Nixon, Mrs. Blank.' I said, 'Well, then, don't vote at all. If your man wins, you'll be out of a job because I won't have any money.' "

The man beside her made murmurs of agreement, and

she said as an afterthought, "But you can't scare them any more."

As I went out, after voting for McGovern, I saw her Cadillac waiting for her with a liveried black chauffeur standing beside it. So you can't be scared any more, I said to him silently. Well, *there's* a little bit of progress.

Saturday, November 11

On the way home from town, where I went to buy a record of Benjamin Britten's *Curlew River* to take to the Crown Prince, I met Frances B. and we came out on the train together. (How many Frans and Franceses I know! The name is almost as common in my generation as the name Elizabeth.) Though it is less than a week before I leave for Japan, we did not talk about that. Now why, I wonder, didn't I say anything about going? I suppose because I have been so afraid of becoming "that old lady who can't talk about anything but Japan—don't get her started."

We talked about getting old. She said that she and her husband spent years building and perfecting a house in Bucks County to which to retire—and then he died two years before he became sixty-five. Not wanting to live alone in the country, she moved to an apartment in Philadelphia. She has friends at Foulkeways, but she says she could not live there because she could not stand going into the dining room every day and seeing all those old women.

Well, there it is. That is the crux of the matter, the depressing part of a retirement community, even the best of them: the segregation of the aged. That and the finality of it. Once in, will one feel trapped?

In the apartment house where I live now almost all the people are old. I don't see them in a dining room, but I do meet them in the elevator, crossing the lobby, sitting in the sun on the lawn. Still, it's not the same. I see Frances's point. I have thought of it myself. But I shall be one of them—at Kendal, if I go in. I shall be as depressing to them as they to me.

Frances spoke of a friend of hers who lived in the same apartment house in which she had lived for many years until the age of ninety-something, then had a brief illness and died in the hospital. "That's what I intend to do," Frances said.

Splendid, if you can. Many people can't. Many land in a nursing home where they don't know anybody, share a room with a stranger—and hope their money will hold out.

There are two basically different ways of approaching what is so mincingly called the Later Years: the stick-it-out-in-the-world policy, and the duck-into-safety policy. The first one sounds so much more gallant, the second slightly craven.

If you have a family, sons and daughters or devoted nieces and nephews, to step in and take responsibility if you fall in the bathroom and break your hip, then you can afford to live dangerously. If you are, as I am, entirely alone, I think you at least examine carefully the second alternative.

I have gone so far as to sign up as a "Founder" of Kendal, the Quaker Retirement Community now being built in Chester County near Longwood Gardens. I have paid half of the entrance fee for a one-bedroom apartment. I can still withdraw in the year that remains before it will be finished.

Sunday, November 12

Fran Fox is back from Maine. She will stay in my apartment while I am in Japan. There aren't many people whom I'd let do that, but Fran has been a dear friend since 1939 or 1940. We went to Meeting together and then on to Marguerite de Angeli's for lunch. Lovely time. She is still writing and illustrating her own books at eighty-three. Her autobiography, *Butter at the Old Price,* came out last year.

San Francisco. Tuesday, November 14

When we were in our thirties, my friend Marjorie and I used to classify old ladies in four categories. We said there were the Whiny Old Ladies, the Bossy Old Ladies, the Fussy Old Ladies, and the Batty Old Ladies. I decided that if I lived so long—which I did not intend to do—I would be a Batty Old Lady. Well, I am.

This morning, as I was doing my final packing and checking at nine-fifteen, preparing to take the train to New York at eleven-fifteen, I could not find my ticket to Japan. Frantically I went through my desk and bureau drawers three times, pulled out bed and file in case the ticket had fallen behind one of them, hunted everywhere. I

30

sat down and attempted to think clearly, to remember where and when I had last had it in my hand. No use. I must have put it in some safe place, now forgotten.

Time pressed. I could not afford to look for it any longer. I telephoned the JAL office in town. They said it would be sticky, but if I got to Kennedy Airport by one o'clock they would give me another ticket. So Fran rushed me to Thirtieth Street Station in the rain, and I got a seat on the 10:46 Metroliner, which was late, a little. In New York there was driving rain and a fierce wind. My porter managed to capture a taxi for me. I told my story to the driver and he got me to Kennedy exactly at one. He said the trip was worth $15 and I agreed that it was ($10.60 on the meter, plus something for tunnel and tip).

The JAL people were kindness itself, as gentle and soothing as if they expected me to be raving mad. I got a new ticket at two and sat in the VIP waiting room, expecting the plane to be called a little before three, when it was scheduled to leave. But what with the wind and rain, the flight was delayed.

Hugh Borton, of the East Asian Institute at Columbia University and former president of Haverford, arrived soon after I did. He and I were the only ones in first class when the plane finally left at five. We dined in state, and later they fixed up the seats so that we could rest. Part of the way across the country I looked out. Below us was a floor of cloud glowing white, and above, a dark blue sky with brilliant stars. San Francisco at last was dramatic, with the looped lights on its bridges.

31

On the bus to the Hilton were two young blacks, one slender with a pointed beard, looking like Stokely Carmichael, the other enormous, collarless, with a round, alive, mustachioed face. The big one spoke with authority and the other man deferred to him.

Their conversation was about the recent hijacking of a plane by three black men, who kept the plane batting back and forth from one city to another, demanding ten million dollars' ransom and finally winding up in Cuba with two million. They thought that most of the hijackers were mentally off but that five per cent were revolutionary. The big man said that if he ever did it he would go to Libya. He said that our government could stop it in a minute if it wanted to, but that it was allowing the hijacking to go on in order to create an atmosphere and frame of mind in people that would make them welcome fascist laws. There was much use of such words as "like" and "man" and "cats" and others that appear so frequently in fiction and the movies. The two men were remarkably knowledgeable about all the hijackings that have taken place, how they were done, who had done them, how much money they got. Should I have been stricken with fear? Somehow it seemed theatrical and unreal; I felt that they were showing off for each other—and perhaps for me.

JAL is putting us up at the Hilton tonight, and tomorrow we fly to Tokyo. This, I gather, is so that we may arrive in Japan rested and ready to enjoy and admire. They don't care how tired we get coming home.

Tokyo. *Thursday, November 16*

Wednesday, November 15, vanished on the international date line.

The trip from the airport into Tokyo, where we are to spend the first two nights before we go on to Kyoto, was a shock to me. Even in the year and a half since I was last here, new speedways have come, new skyscrapers risen into the sky, traffic has multiplied, more old landmarks have disappeared. Even the great seventeenth-century walls of the Imperial Palace grounds seem to have shrunk, contained within the crisscrossing lines of the new elevated highways.

Tané Matsumura and the others who came to meet me have gone. Fruit and flowers bloom on table and desk in my room at the Okura Hotel. I have a balcony looking out on a pool with a small fountain, and Tokyo Tower, a little higher than the Eiffel Tower, thrusts itself high into the sky, looking like a huge furled umbrella with golden lights for ribs and a scarlet tip. Nearby a high-rise addition to the hotel is going up, and concrete mixers and mechanical shovels are rattling and screaming. I suppose they have to work at night when the narrow streets are empty of traffic.

Friday, November 17

Sunny and surprisingly warm in the morning, cloudy in the afternoon. Early in the morning I heard birds in the trees beyond my balcony. I got up and looked out; they were *onagas*, the striking long-tailed blue magpies.

33

After breakfast I called my friend and former student Asako, and we went for a walk around the neighborhood, looking in on Fujimicho Church. This is a well-known Presbyterian church built in the late-nineteenth-century pseudo-Gothic style approved by missionaries. We also visited a small old temple with black tiled roofs, under tall trees, and a bronze bell in a cage. Finally we stopped in at a small weathered wooden shop with a blue *noren*—divided curtain—over the doorway and the name, Chimaki-ya, carved on a wooden sign. Asako bought some *chimaki*, a sort of soft bean jelly wrapped in bamboo leaves, which we took home to her smart modern apartment and ate with very good tea. In all the noise and glare of modern Tokyo there are bits of the old to be found tucked away in the mazes of small streets that still survive.

Asako, product of the Peeresses School and Bryn Mawr College, looks well and at peace with herself. She is greatly pleased with the house which she has built at Hayama with money she inherited from her father, who died a year or so ago. I am to go and stay with her there later on, and see the view of Sagami Bay beneath her windows and Mount Fuji soaring into the sky over the water. She buys freedom at the price of loneliness and finds it a bargain.

Saturday, November 18, 4 a.m.

Awake at four in the morning. In my window the Tower is a broken series of green lights in the sky, then a pause of darkness, then a shaft of golden lights jutting high with a red one pulsing at the top.

I had dinner last night in a Chinese restaurant with three of the top administrators of the International Christian University and Hugh Borton and Dr. Paul Gregory of the J. I. C. U. Foundation Board* in New York. Most of the talk was about money for the university. The I. C. U. wants to raise money in the United States, which is increasingly difficult because Japan has a better trade balance than we have and businessmen do not see why she should not support her own schools. On the other hand, Bryn Mawr would like to get—as Harvard has—a large grant from Japan. Both I. C. U. and Bryn Mawr would welcome help from me, and I am useless when it comes to raising money.

A red light runs up the shaft of the Tower.

I wonder why I ever came to this affair. The Japanese P. E. N. is spending so much money on me, and for what? I am not an expert on Japan. The real working members of the Japan Center, who may not be the least bit concerned with explaining Japanese culture to an international crowd, are probably getting on with their novels about foot fetishes and fellatio and the like. Some dull papers will be read to sparse audiences and laboriously translated by girls in a high room above the auditorium, while the real fun goes on in small groups gathering to drink and swap stories. There will be some loudly exasperated Frenchman making a fuss that nobody understands. In the evenings I shall see small parties forming and going off to unnamed delights. In the end, too late, I shall prob-

*Japanese International Christian University Foundation.

35

ably find some congenial mouse. I wish I were at home. I am hungry and cross. I shall eat a banana from my fruit basket.

8:45 a.m. Now, having bathed, dressed, and breakfasted, I am much less poor-spirited.

The *Japan Times*, one of three English-language newspapers in Japan, is a more interesting paper than those I read at home. There are few advertisements, and the news coverage is broad and varied. The Saturday Supplement is given over to the P. E. N. Conference, and I am ashamed of my early-morning petulance. There will be very distinguished people here indeed. The first plenary session in Kyoto includes Prince Mikasa; Dr. Edwin O. Reischauer, our former ambassador to Japan, now professor of Asian Studies at Harvard and the author of excellent books on Japan; Kojiro Yoshikawa, President Emeritus of Kyoto University. There will be sections on literature, art, music, drama, as well as all sorts of entertainment and two "Academic Tours."

I found in the *Japan Times* an annotated list of the week's best sellers. Two books deal with aging. *Kakotsuno Hito* (The Ecstatic Ones) by Sawako Ariyoshi is described: "The authoress analyzes the way of life of elderly people with special reference to the childish 'spiritual raptures' that she says they experience during their long years in retirement. She suggests that their ecstasies might have been affected by mental deterioration." Hmm.

Kainoroku (A Warning to the Aged) is "an essay on the

path which Akiko Sono wrote at her thirty-seventh birthday in an attempt to prepare for the second half of her life. The authoress presents her views on the meaning of life and especially the spiritual maturity that may be attained only when one's life draws to a close." I know people who are spiritually mature at thirty-seven, if she means what I think she does.

The increased interest in aging on the part of younger people is something new and it may have a strong effect on the generation of older people thirty years from now. They form an even larger percentage of the population than we do, and their grandchildren, born of the ecologically aware, will be fewer. If they begin now to think about what they will be when they are old, to develop lively and enduring interests, to insure their health by enlightened diet and reasonable exercise, if they are politically foresighted enough to legislate for the needs of the old, then surely there will be fewer derelicts sitting in dreary rows in nursing-home corridors. Perhaps even senility can be prevented.

10 p.m. The Opening Ceremony of the Conference took place at seven in the ballroom, which was provided with rows of chairs, a stage, gold screens, flowers. My heart beat fast as I watched the Crown Prince and Princess Michiko come in to the music of the "Kimigayo" played by court musicians in ancient, brilliant costume. I love the "Kimigayo"; it is a slow, solemn, and beautiful national anthem. Still more I loved seeing the Crown Prince in ac-

37

tion in public as Crown Prince, as I so seldom do. For four years, from 1946 to 1950, he was my pupil. Since then he has been my friend. I have met him in his palace or in my own little house in Philadelphia, in the White House or in hotels in the United States on his visits there. I thought of that day in October 1946 when I first came to Japan to teach him English and incidentally Western civilization. He was twelve years old, nearly thirteen, such a sturdy, honest, earnest, lovable little boy. All around us then lay the ruins of Tokyo, miles of burned-over land and make-shift wooden shelters, with here and there scarred brick or concrete buildings that had survived the B-29 fire raids. Now, still boyish-looking at thirty-eight, he has a bearing both confident and modest. Married to a lovely young woman, of his own choice, he has three children—two boys and a girl. Princess Michiko, gliding behind him, was beautiful in a gray and white and gold kimono with a tangerine-colored obi.

Including the Crown Prince's, there were six speeches, most of them longer than they were supposed to be. (I saw the working program, with each item planned down to the last second.) One old boy, who was obviously popular and privileged, got wound up and ran on unconscionably. Mr. Serisawa, the president of the Japan Center, pointedly stood up in his place at the left of the platform. He and others coughed. No use. At length he sent a messenger with a note. The messenger, a uniformed, white-gloved hotel employee, walked doubled over, to indicate, no doubt, that he was invisible. The old boy made some remark that elicited laughter and went on. ("They want me to stop, but I haven't finished," someone afterward told me he said.) Several minutes later he finished. When the President of the French Academy, who came next, went over his time, the old boy coughed loudly. The Crown Prince came last. He read his exactly timed speech clearly and easily, looking up at the audience from time to time, while Princess Michiko sat motionless and attentive, her eyes never leaving his face.

The guests of honor and a few others, fifteen altogether, were invited to a smaller room afterward to meet the Crown Prince and Princess. They moved around the circle, chatting a little with each one of us. I saw them a year and a half ago when I was in Tokyo, and I am to see them later when I come back from Kyoto.

Afterward there were cocktails and a buffet for eight hundred. I did not stay long, just long enough to meet a few whom I wanted to see. Princess Takako, now Mrs. Hisanaga Shimazu, very slender and smart in a slim black dress with spectacular pearls, hailed me cordially and said she would be at the Conference for part of the time. The Crown Prince's youngest sister, whom I still see in my mind as a seven-year-old with shining black bangs and a yellow wool dress, has grown into a lovely—and refreshingly informal—young woman of the world.

Kyoto. Sunday, November 19

From Tokyo to Kyoto, in what Westerners call the Bullet Train. It is a miracle of speed, cleanliness, and comfort, and I am envious, remembering our own dirty, dilatory trains. There was color in the trees along the way; the rice fields were flooded, rice sheaves hung on racks to dry, and bright-colored *futon* (quilts) were everywhere spread out in the sunshine. The mountains on the horizon were hazy.

At the Miyako Hotel the view from my window is lovely: old houses on a narrow lane below, a green mountain in the distance with a temple among the trees at its foot.

There was a dull cocktail party, at which I talked to the same people I'd already talked to without saying much, but on the way out I ran into the Gotos. They are old friends, poets who have taught the Crown Prince. We had dinner together, along with Miss Reiko Tsukimura, who teaches at the University of Minnesota and who will read a paper on Yasunari Kawabata, the Nobel Prize winner, on the twenty-second.

It is a source of shame and frustration to me that I have never learned to speak Japanese beyond the barest necessity for getting about. I was immensely fortunate, when I was here from 1946 to 1950, in having Tané always with me to interpret. For this Conference the P. E. N. has provided a secretary and, if needed, an interpreter for each of the special guests. Mine is a delightful young woman, a graduate student at Keio University named Fusako Kobayashi. The generosity and forethought of the Japanese are extraordinary.

Monday, November 20

At 6 a.m. the hills I see from my window are dark, and

40

there are lights still in the lowland between here and the mountains. But the traffic noises have begun, the rush of autos on the road and the roll of streetcars heavy on the rails. Slowly, at long intervals, I hear the sound of a temple bell, musical and evocative, with the rich depth that comes from its being struck not by a metal clapper but by a heavy beam of wood.

At eight-thirty I set off on foot by myself to Nanzenji, the great Zen Buddhist temple. After crossing two main roads, I walked down a narrow street between whitewashed and tile-roofed stone walls. A stream gushed along one side; ferns grew between the rocks; pine trees and scarlet maples showed over the walls. Here and there a driveway curved between bushes to what was obviously a mansion. Then on the left came the temple Konchiin, an offshoot of Nanzenji. A wooden board outside, put up by Kyoto City, tells in both English and Japanese of the age of the temple and the treasures within. I looked in from the gate and saw a booth where tickets and postcards were sold, flanked by a screaming-red Coca-Cola dispenser. Shuddering, I fled to the main entrance to Nanzenji, where men were sweeping the wide asphalt approach in preparation for the day. Schoolboys in navy-blue serge uniforms came hurrying by.

On the way home, waiting for the traffic light to turn, were two young men: an American, sandy-haired, round-faced, freckled; and a Japanese in a dark blue suit, with shining, thick black hair, who turned out to be a Buddhist priest. The American said, "Are you Mrs. Vining?" Then he told me his name and that he taught Japanese Literature

41

at Kansas State University. When he was in high school, he read *Windows for the Crown Prince*, and because of that he decided to make Japanese Studies his career. He is a member of the P. E. N. Conference.

It is rather frightening to think of the unknown lives that one has touched. One hears only about those where the touch has been beneficent, but what of those ·whom one may, equally unconsciously, have harmed?

Later. The new Conference Center is beautiful, both in its setting of mountains, garden, and reflecting pool and in the elegant halls within. In the main auditorium, equipped with earphones for simultaneous translation, we listened to the speeches of the first plenary session.

Prince Mikasa, the Emperor's youngest brother, was there not as a prince, so said the President of the P. E. N. in his introduction, but as a scholar in his own right. A slender man in his late fifties with a dark birdlike profile like his grandmother's (the Empress Dowager), Prince Mikasa is a popular professor of Mideastern History in a women's college in Tokyo. When he visited Philadelphia a few years ago, the leading archaeologists of the University of Pennsylvania all turned out for him. During the last year I was in Japan—1950—he used to come to my house once a week for English conversation. He came to me, not I to him. Sometimes he drove up in his tiny Datsun; sometimes he came by train and walked over from the station, carrying his brief case. He was always refreshingly frank and outspoken and utterly without pomposity of any kind.

I was eager to hear what he would say to the four hundred or so Japanologists assembled from forty-two countries.

He was not, he began, an expert on Japan; his field was the history of the Eastern Mediterranean, and to ask him to talk on Japan was like asking an oculist to deliver a baby. He told how it was that he had gone into the field he did, and this I had not heard before.

He was a graduate of the War College, where he studied the history of war and was told about Japan's greatness and the necessity of war. When the war came, he was sent to Nanking—and there he saw that war was entirely different from what he had supposed. And so when he got out of the army, he decided to study the early history of man, to try to find out why men were as they were and what made for violence and war. All this, of course, was filtered through the simultaneous interpreters in their workroom high above us. He did not, so far as I could discover, tell if he had found the secret of man's violence.

Dr. Reischauer had come for just two days, and even before this session was over he was slipping away to get a plane back to the United States. He is immensely well liked in Japan and has done for our country what no other ambassador has done, except perhaps Joseph Grew in his ten years here before World War II. I remember asking Dr. Shinzo Koizumi about Reischauer and getting the enthusiastic reply, "Oh, he is splendid. We can talk to him. He *listens!*" Dr. Reischauer spoke today of Japan's fear that her culture might be lost through modernization—a fear which he felt was groundless—and of Japan's influence on

43

the West. The effect of Japanese architecture is obvious; he pointed out that seventeenth-century Japanese art has the worldwide attraction today that Renaissance art has lost.

In the afternoon session, which was devoted to *Genji Monogatari*, the great eleventh-century novel by Lady Murasaki, Mrs. Myoka Goto, the poet, was the star. She was substituting at the last minute for a Japanese woman novelist who had been taken ill. Small, dressed all in gray, with a gray toque on her brown (not black) hair, looking very feminine with her big eyes and gentle expression, she began in the old-fashioned Japanese woman's way with apologies and self-depreciation, whereupon several men in the back of the hall got up and left. But once she got into her stride she was excellent, and I thought she more than held her own among the other speakers.

A blind novelist named Seiichi Funabashi, who evidently commands great respect in Japan, though he is unknown, because untranslated, outside the country, made a long and scholarly address. The part of it that caught my interest especially was his pointing out how down the ages Lady Murasaki's novel has been doctored—by the Confucians, by the nationalists, and, during the last war, by the militarists—all to make it morally instructive. The relations of Genji with his stepmother were actually not allowed to be known to the general reader in Japan until after World War II. No wonder I have heard English-speaking Japanese say that they preferred to read it in Arthur Waley's brilliant and unexpurgated translation! I must never, I tell myself, relax my opposition to censorship, no matter how horrified I may be by what gets printed in the excesses of freedom. If even a great novel is subject to distortion by the censors, what would they not do to much more awkward and necessary truths?

At lunch I sat beside a Brazilian diplomat who assured me earnestly that in Brazil they care nothing about money or rank, only about each individual and his gifts. And I had dinner with a delightful Hungarian woman who speaks sixteen languages and who, having recently spent two months in the United States, was outspokenly envious of the freedom we enjoy.

Wednesday, November 22

After the morning session on the novelists Kobo Abe, Yukie Mishima, and Yasunari Kawabata, I took Fusako Kobayashi, my secretary, pro tem, and Kayoko Horiguchi, who studied library science in Philadelphia several years ago, with me in the car assigned to me to see Abbess Komatsu at Jakkōin Temple. The ride up the valley among the tall mountains was as lovely in the fall coloring as it was last year in cherry-blossom time—and today it was not raining.

There were crowds of sightseers in this small old temple established nearly eight centuries ago to take care of an empress fleeing from defeat in the wars of the Heike and the Taira. Ever since then it has provided an abbacy for some spare—or dedicated—woman of the Imperial Family. Komatsu San, the present abbess, is a woman of brains and presence, about fifty yeras old, whose devotion to the cause

45

of peace is known and respected. When a delegation of seventeen top-ranking Japanese Buddhists made a trip to Europe a few years ago to visit religious centers, including the Vatican, she was the only woman among them.

Last year Dorothy Dessau, my fellow Bryn Mawrtyr, who lives and works in Kyoto, brought me here, and Komatsu San and I formed one of those delicate but deep relationships that are perhaps the stronger for being so largely wordless. Komatsu San told me then (through an interpreter) of her love of peace and her lifelong desire to work for it, of her coming to the temple as a little girl of ten, of her education at Kyoto schools and a Buddhist university on Mount Hiei. I was happy to be able to see her again and to introduce the two young Japanese women to her.

Komatsu San, wearing purple silk damask with a white headdress, received us in her own quarters, then took us to the part of the temple that is not open to the public. It is a tiny place with a beautiful view. Below the *roka* (small balcony) stretched the narrow valley and the steep mountains, not distant layer on layer as at home, but a nearby presence. Through a cleft was a view of a slightly more distant peak, the maples glowing scarlet on its flank. From another room we saw a tiny pond, framed in trees, with a pattern of scarlet leaves on its green surface, and from still another room a small court where two old women in baggy trousers and towels tied around their heads were filling baskets with leaves and weeds.

Inside this small temple building one is wholly unaware

46

of the restless lines of sightseers outside. We were shown some of the temple's treasures: a pitted piece of wood from the boat in which a long-ago emperor was drowned; the straw sandals worn by Emperor Go-Shirakawa when he visited Kanreimon, the first abbess; the famous paintings by Tosson, and so on. We had ceremonial tea, served by the abbess's young assistant, and persimmons and chestnut cakes. We exchanged conversation and compliments with the abbess. She gave me two *shikishi*—square gilt-edged cards—on which she had this morning written poems that she composed especially for me. I told her about the two young women with me, and she took the snapshot of Kayoko's children in her hands and, holding it up to the level of her forehead, prayed for the children. I gave her a book of photographs of the United States—beautiful indeed but highly selective—and she prayed for my health and for peace in the world.

When we left, she accompanied us all the way down the hill to the car, pointing out to us along the way the wooden plaques on which she had caused to be inscribed passages from the sutras recommending peace and a quiet heart to visitors. The tourists, however, were not impressed by them. Going down the steep slope, we were nearly swept off our feet by a band of schoolgirls who apparently did not even see the abbess in her purple robe and white veil.

My two Japanese companions were thrilled by the experience and talked of it all the way back to the city: of the charm of Komatsu San, the uplifted feeling that they got

47

from the meeting with her, the fact that for the first time a Buddhist temple—and in their school excursions they had visited many—had given these two Christian Japanese a sense of worship and spiritual meaning. Japanese Christians, I find, are often less open to Buddhism than Americans are.

Thursday, November 23

Since I've been here I have had several talks with Japanese women about the modern women who have been most influential in moving Japan forward out of feudalism, and every time the name of the poet Akiko Yosano has come up. Yesterday at the bookstand in the Conference Center I looked up her poems in an anthology. The translations were obviously poor, but I came upon one poem that I liked. The moving last line, "I beg you not to die," was addressed, I assumed, to her lover.

This morning, breakfasting with Dr. Joyce Ackroyd of Australia, who specializes in Tokugawa History and modern poetry, I asked her about Akiko Yosano. Akiko Yosano was, it seems, a "modern Heian woman." That is, she went forward by retreating to the mood and spirit of the eleventh century, when Japanese women—Lady Murasaki, Sei Shonagon, and others—had position and influence. The poem that I liked was addressed not to a lover but to her brother, a soldier in the Russo-Japanese War. To beg him not to die was an expression of independence and courage at a time when the overwhelming weight of Japanese opinion was that a soldier's greatest desire, as well as his duty, was to die for the Emperor. Japanese women ever since have recognized this poet as a rebel and a spokesman for freedom.

It was another sunny, cold day, though by evening it had clouded over and the wind was sharp. The morning was taken up with the last plenary session, which was a winding-up of the academic show with a good speech by Dr. Charles Fahs. In the afternoon there were two farewell parties.

The one held at the Nomura Garden was considered more desirable, for the notation on the program said, "Limited to 200 guests. By invitation only." I received a note telling me to go to the other one, at the Conference Hall. A big feeling of status had built up. People said to me, "You're going to the Nomura Garden, of course," and when I said no, they looked surprised or pitying. Whatever the reason—and I am sure that there was a sound, practical reason and that no disrespect to me was intended—I found that I honestly did not care, especially after I got to the party. I flatter myself that I have absorbed enough Zen to be more concerned with the thing-in-itself than with the way it may appear from the outside.

I am convinced that I was at the better party, for it must have been cold in the garden, and you sit still for a long time at a Noh play, which was the feature of the Nomura Garden party. At the Center we had a cocktail party in a warm dining room overlooking the reflecting pool and the mountains. Then, as we watched from the great glass windows, a colorful and dramatic dance was staged on the terrace. A hero in a brilliant costume fought with and slew four wonderfully fierce dragons with long, lashing tails, and then pulled the imperial sword from the tail of the last one. As the sky darkened behind the dancers, fires flared in fire pots on the edge of the terrace against the black line of the hills. The music was exciting. At the end of the dance the flares were put out and there was a spectacular show of fireworks: showers of fire, red and gold, set pieces such as Niagara Falls pouring gold down the sky, and at the end "P. E. N. Sayonara" spelled out in letters of flame. The whole program was utterly enchanting.

Mr. Serisawa, the President of the Japan Chapter of the P. E. N., was there to say good-by to us, and we went back to the hotel through the dark old city.

The one frustrating thing about this Conference is that one sees people, has a pleasant or stimulating talk with them, and then does not see them again. But I have enjoyed especially the Fahses, Miss Reiko Tsukimura, Dr. Joyce Ackroyd, Dr. Kenneth Yasuda, who teaches at Indiana University and translates Japanese poetry into English, and, of course, the Gotos.

I've also had pleasant encounters with Miss G. D. Ivanova, the Russian writer. We've met again and again in the elevator. The first morning she said to me, in English, "My English is terrible. Let us speak Japanese." And I replied to her, in Japanese, "My Japanese is worse." So we communicated through "body language"—smiles and nods and gestures—and shared, I am sure, more friendly warmth than we could have conveyed through any exchange of ideas.

Tomorrow to Nara.

Friday, November 24

Our party yesterday was, as I suspected, more fun than the other one. The Nomura Garden was cold and windy; there were booths for Japanese food, and geishas doing their rather boring little routines, and then the guests went into a small, unheated hall for a long Noh play. But this was considered the *erai* (VIP) affair, and I saw again, as I have seen so often before, the foreigner's uneasiness in Japan lest he fail to get the top treatment. It took me back, too, to the time of the Occupation, when all was rank and there was much jockeying for position.

The last two days are to be devoted to sightseeing, and I opted for Nara rather than the Toba Peninsula and the pearl farm. Nothing could ever come up to my visit to it in 1947, when the old Pearl King himself was living and Tané and I had lunch with him in his small Japanese house atop the hill with a spectacular view.

Because the Matsushita Company was a large contributor to the Conference, we were taken on the way to Nara to see their main plant in Osaka. There was a vast difference between this enormous, shining, automated establishment and the shabby factories struggling amid the rubble that I visited in March 1950, but the drill was the same: gathering in a large boardroom, tea, speeches, a tour of inspection, and a return to the boardroom for Coca-

Cola, speeches, and presents. We saw all the TV sets, from one you can carry on your wrist to a large and elaborate affair that takes your picture and presents you with a print on the spot.

Men and girls in smart delft-blue uniforms work at long benches eight hours a day, five days a week, with five minutes off in the morning, forty-five minutes for lunch, and five minutes off in the afternoon. They are given all sorts of fringe benefits from a paternalistic company, and they have, we were told, a high sense of *esprit de corps* and loyalty to the company. Mr. Konosuke Matsushita himself is a very enlightened man who promotes world understanding through the publication of a magazine, *PHP*, which stands for peace, happiness, and prosperity.

Nara has its old magic, and I saw the places I have loved and some bits I had not seen before. One of the moments that most symbolized for me the essence of Japan was a bare tree with a few persimmons against the blue sky. Fusako, who is still with me, quoted a poem about two persimmons and the Hōryūji Temple, and while the bus was waiting for passengers, she ran to a stand nearby and bought some persimmons for me.

Saturday, November 25

During these two beautiful days in Nara everybody has been much more relaxed and friendly, as if a strain were over. I've enjoyed talking with some people whom I did not even see at the Conference Center. A large and smiling Indian, Dr. Lokesh Chandra, presented me with a little wooden pin in the shape of an oak leaf with an acorn and a mushroom dangling from it. "It came from the Soviet Union," he said with a teasing smile, as if he expected me to fling it away in horror. But I am charmed with it—and with him.

I have enjoyed, too, Dr. Ury Eppstein, the young Israeli musicologist whom Fusako picked up, who specializes in *gagaku*, the ancient Japanese court music, and teaches at the University of Tel Aviv. His father was born in Philadelphia, but Dr. Eppstein has never been to the United States. At dinner Dr. Eppstein spoke of the limitations of the Conference, of any such gathering: of the absurdity of a man's reading a paper to an audience that already has a copy of that paper in its hands, and then of the feebleness of the discussions that follow. Other people have commented on the poor discussions, on the lengthy questions difficult to summarize, the almost invariable answer, "As I said in my paper"—as if the speaker were confined by his paper or had poured his whole resources into it. Or else the question was jejune, betraying that the questioner had not really listened to the speech. The value of the Conference for most people lay in the personal contacts, the individual discussions in corridors and lobbies and over meals, and in the published proceedings that will come later. It is to be a very handsome book, Fusako says, each volume to cost thousands of yen. All the papers will be included, not just those that were read, not just the best; those that were taken out of the barrel in order for the author to be admitted to the Conference will be there too.

53

After dinner another young Israeli joined us, and soon I left them with Fusako. The young men gather around her like flies around honey.

The International House, Tokyo. Sunday, November 26

The Conference is over and I am on my own, staying for the next two weeks in this delightful club where everyone is cordial and informal and I can see my old friends again. The Conference was a great experience, though I was an observer, not a participant, and therefore never really part of it, and though I had always the uneasy feeling that I was making no contribution that could in any way justify the amount of money the P.E.N. was spending on me.

This morning, when I had breakfast with one of my Conference acquaintances, I asked her about her feelings about the Conference. She is burdened by the extravagant generosity of the Japan P.E.N., sees no way to repay it, feels that the *on* (debt of honor) incurred will hamper her in speaking about Japan and that she has been, in a sense, prostituted. She was troubled by the poverty of the discussions, felt that there was much academic social climbing and that the nationals all clung together, the British, the Americans, the Russians, the Japanese, all associating with their own kind. She spoke of seasoned conference-goers who knew how to shut other people out. Nonetheless, she said she enjoyed the Conference immensely and was filled with admiration for the Japanese gift for planning and carrying out such a party and for their generosity. She seemed to have felt even more out of things than I did, possibly because of male chauvinism in the academic world. She struck me as being very intelligent, almost painfully honest, sensitive and disarming.

As I watched her talk and enjoyed the play of her expression, I realized suddenly that the thirty years or so advantage in age that I have over her is in real ways an advantage. At seventy I can afford to be an observer. I am out of the struggle. I no longer have to prove anything. I can enjoy the thing-in-itself, whatever it is, without regard to the prestige value or the effect that it may have on my career.

Of course part of my advantage stems from the fact that I am a writer and not a college professor. I have never felt discriminated against in the writing world because I am a woman. I have the same kind of book contracts that men have and the same chance with the reading public. But in the academic world a woman, even a brilliant woman, has to struggle against determined, if concealed, opposition to make her way from an assistant to an associate professorship, and women who are full professors are a very small minority.

Monday, November 27

Sunny and breezy and crisp. Sitting at breakfast this morning, I looked out at the garden, with its tiny brook and stone lanterns, its wheat-colored *susuki* (like our pampas grass) swaying in the wind, and saw two gray wagtails teetering across the brown lawn.

At ten Tomi Koizumi, Dr. Shinzo Koizumi's widow, and her daughter Kayo Akiyama arrived, bearing an enchanting flower arrangement and a box of *marrons glacés*. We talked long about many things, including Tomi's husband. How I miss Shinzo! He was one of the great Japanese men whom I knew well. Former university president, writer on many subjects, my colleague (his term) in the Crown Prince's education, and my boss (my term), he was Japan's postwar conscience. Offered several distinguished honors, he would accept only the Cultural Medal. It is six years since his death at the age of seventy-eight.

Tomi, at seventy-five, is as flowerlike as ever, with the depth and humor that make her so delightful a companion. When I was young, I used to collect married couples who seemed to me to be exhibits in favor of marriage. Now I collect old persons who are good advertisements for age, and Tomi Koizumi is one of a distinguished list. She still lives in the house she and Shinzo built, with her daughter Tae and Tae's husband in a small house on the same ground, and the Akiyamas nearby. This is an ideal way for a widow to spend her last years. It's what we all would like, and with all my heart I hope that nothing will happen to change it for Tomi.

Tuesday, November 28

Miss Keiko Hani came today to have lunch with me, looking a bit plumper and older and a little careworn. Since her mother's death she has carried on her mother's school, Jiyu Gakuen, by herself—no slight burden. And after all, she is twenty-six years older now than the young woman whom I first met in 1947.

We talked about her mother—and what a story there is in the life of Motoko Hani! After lunch Miss Hani invited me to go with her to Ueno Museum to see the special Rimpa exhibit there now. She had her car, and it took us forty-five minutes to drive to Ueno along the crowded length of the Ginza and Kanda. Everything looked new and clean to me after the shabbiness and destruction of the postwar period.

The Rimpa exhibit at the Ueno was a very fine one. Case after case was filled with screens, scrolls, lacquer boxes, with bold Korin designs and an endless variety of flowers. At one point we looked out of the museum window and saw a pond, pines, and a small temple enclosed by a stone wall, all very old and traditional. Beyond the wall tall blocks of buildings thrust their concrete whiteness into the sky.

"They look like tombstones," said Miss Hani sadly. "Tombstones for old Japan."

Tané and Yukio and Yukio's seventeen-year-old daughter, Emi, came to take me to dinner. Mrs. Takaki met us at the restaurant, Zaburo, where we had a room to ourselves. Dear Tatsuo Takaki, she is high on my list of advertisements for old age. She was one of my first friends in Japan. At the first audience I had with the Emperor and Empress and the Crown Prince, two days after I got here in October 1946, Mrs. Takaki interpreted. I remember so well walking with her down the long corridor to the audience chamber, feeling so far away from home and so keyed up, and being aware of her calm, warm, friendly support, being attracted by her beauty,. Now she is well over eighty and has suffered a slight stroke, so that her speech comes very slowly. She is not frustrated by the difficulty; she persists, quite calmly, until what she wants to say gets said. She has had tragedies in her life—her husband's death in an automobile accident, the recent death of a promising young grandson—but she has won serenity.

Whenever I have a meal in a Japanese restaurant and see the beauty and variety of the china, I think of the horror of one of my young Japanese friends when she first went to an American restaurant and was obliged to drink out of a thick white cup and eat from cheap and common but durable plates. At Zaburo we had *shabu-shabu*, boiling broth in a copper pot in the center of the table. We dipped paper-thin pieces of beef into the broth and swished them back and forth—*"shabu-shabu."* Later vegetables, such as Chinese cabbage and green beans, were added. Finally the broth, which was delicious, was ladled into bowls and we drank it.

At the end of the meal the proprietor came in with a present for me (a teapot), and we left amid a multitude of bows—the proprietor and all the waitresses (in black kimonos with sea-green obis) lined up in two rows to see us off. This is really amazing: after so many years so much excitement over a teacher. How Violet would laugh! I wish I could tell her. She used to say that someday—in a hundred years perhaps—I should certainly be in a Kabuki play, tragically in love with—whom?

Thursday, November 30

From my balcony in the mornings I can see Mount Fuji, faint and snow-clad in the distant sky. By ten o'clock or so the mountain has disappeared, hidden by the polluted air of Tokyo.

There is a report that International House will be closed for two years, while the present building is torn down and one of many stories built to replace it. Land is so fantastically expensive in Tokyo now and taxes so high that a three-story building is not economically feasible. So another delightful small place will be enlarged and spoiled. I feel sad.

Friday, December 1

Brilliantly sunny and cold. Tané and I went to Tsuda College by taxi, train, and another taxi. Japan's new wealth shows in the trains, in the new bright subways with trains running every few minutes, and in the handsome new buses, where smartly uniformed young women help people on and off. I should hate to have to use public transportation at rush hours, when, I am told, there are pushers to pack people in, but in the middle of the day the subway is clean and convenient and much faster than private cars. The traffic jams in Tokyo are beyond anything we know.

The library at Tsuda College was designed by one of Japan's great architects and set among pine trees. It is a beautiful building, an architect's, but not a librarian's, dream. The dramatic glass sides let in far too much sun, making the large reading room unbearably hot; the great windows must be expensively curtained. In contrast, the workroom, where the books must be ordered, processed, and catalogued, is tiny and dark and cold. This happens in American libraries, too.

Michi Nakamura, assistant librarian, a Drexel Library School graduate and an old friend, had gathered together material about Miss Ume Tsuda, the founder, for me, and for about two hours I worked happily with it before it was time to go to the president's house for lunch.

Taki Fujita, who was at Bryn Mawr when I was, has succeeded Ai Hoshino, president of Tsuda when I used to lecture once a month on American Literature and Violet taught English Composition once a week, back in the 1940s. Taki had a bad motor accident last year and is still on crutches. Because she was in the hospital so long, she has had little chance to know this year's freshmen and now is catching up by inviting thirty of them at a time to lunch with her. Tané and I were included in today's party. We all sat in a circle with Miss Fujita in the center, and each of us was given, to my amazement, a pasteboard box with Colonel Sanders' familiar face on it. Inside were fried chicken, rolls, and cole slaw. Kentucky fried chicken, it seems, has taken Japan by storm. Tea was also provided, and a mandarin orange.

It all reminded me, apart from Colonel Sanders, of course, of President Thomas's receptions at Bryn Mawr, when we sat in a great circle around the fireplace, and Miss Thomas, in the center, an imposing—and indeed terrifying—figure, would say ponderously, "Now, what shall we talk about?" Taki Fujita at seventy-five is also an impressive figure. She is somewhat heavyset; her short, bobbed hair is black with a sprinkling of gray; her honest, strong face is alive with interest and humor.

She reminisced a bit about Tsuda's history, then went around the circle asking each girl where she came from, drawing her out to talk and ask questions. The subject of coeducation was handled in a rather gingerly fashion, I thought, but the girls obviously enjoyed the occasion, and there was laughter from time to time.

I had another period of work in the library and then returned to Taki's for tea. One of the younger professors told me that she had been in Violet's Composition class in 1949. She has never forgotten that one day she was caught in Violet's class doing her homework for another course. Violet said to her gently, "It's too much for you to do homework and classwork too." She never did it again. Violet enjoyed that class and for years kept samples of the students' compositions, both for their intrinsic interest and for their quaint English. I wonder if this was the girl who said to her, "I remorse my mistakes."

After tea Michi drove Tané and me back to Tokyo in her little car. The road where I remember farms is now all built up, but once between the buildings we had a glimpse of a line of blue mountains and above them, huge, white, draped with a streamer of cloud, Fuji soared majestic, dwarfing all else. We parked the car in Shinjuku, where there is now a spacious underground city with shops and walks surrounding the clean and well-lit parking lot. From there we took an elevator to a restaurant run by some people from Kyoto, where all was simple and harmonious bamboo and pale wood and modern lights. There was a koto player and light, delicious food.

The whole district of Shinjuku, Tané said, is now a gathering place for young people. This is where her step-children come for clothes and amusements. Along the side of the station buildings for perhaps a hundred yards young people were camped, waiting for the ticket office to open tomorrow morning, when they could buy tickets to ski resorts for the beginning of the Christmas holidays. They had spread out newspapers, blankets, coats, sometimes an air mattress; they had food and thermos bottles, and there they lay, heads to the wall, feet to the passersby, by ones and twos, a boy and a girl, two girls, two boys. The evening was clear, but the air was sharp.

This was a different Shinjuku from the one I used to drive through almost daily from 1946 through 1950. Then the prewar buildings were damaged and shabby; there were gaps and empty lots. The streets were dirty. On the top of one building there was a large and faded signboard advertising "Kiss-Me Lipstick."

After my happy audience this afternoon with Her Majesty—who does not change, though the Palace grows steadily grander and more formal—Miss Taira, my dear old flower-arrangement teacher, Tané, and Michi Nakamura came to dinner at International House with me. Miss Taira is seventy-five now and feeling her age, though she still hops all over Tokyo from morning till night, teaching flower arrangement, attending meetings, doing charming things for her friends.

While we were having dinner, the windows began to rattle and the floor to shudder. The waiters all rushed to open the glass sliding doors onto the terrace, in case they should jam and we not be able to get out. The tremors went on for what seemed a long time, and people sat looking at each other apprehensively. Earthquakes are alarming in this city of immense crowds, new skyscrapers, and subways; nobody pretends not to be worried about what might happen.

Tuesday, December 5

It is hard for me to believe, but it has happened again: I have been entertained as an honored and cherished guest by the Crown Prince and Princess Michiko.

In the drawing room with the goldfish tank set into the wall, where I have been before, they were waiting for me, with the Crown Prince's elder sister, now Mrs. Takatsukasa. A little later their two sons came in, Prince Hiro, tall and slender, noticeably more mature than he was a year and a half ago, an intelligent and graceful boy, and seven-year-old Prince Aya, bright-faced and uninhibited. He crawled around his elder brother like a bear, punched him, lay on his chair with his feet in the air, uttered squeals, and generally showed off. When rebuked by Princess Michiko, "Aya!" and by Prince Akihito, sternly, "AYA!", he said disarmingly, "But I am excited!" Princess Michiko turned to me, smiling. "He is our lively one," she said. And what a joy it was to see, this happy, natural child, surrounded by love and humor, unburdened by the stiff formality that had imprisoned his father's childhood. Three-year-old Princess Saya was in bed with a cold, and so I did not see her.

After some talk and my small presents, the little boys said good-by politely and withdrew. A delicious Japanese dinner was brought in, and over it the talk ranged far and wide: to Afghanistan and the royal couple's recent visit there, Spain, the P.E.N. Conference, India, and Bangladesh. Dr. Chandra, who gave me the Soviet pin, had spent an afternoon with the Crown Prince and had told him that he had seen me at the Conference. Dr. Chandra is a very big shot indeed, both as a scholar and a statesman.

Princess Michiko told me a lovely story about little Princess Saya. Last summer when they were all at Karuizawa in the mountains where I enjoyed four summers, the child was lonely and longed for playmates. They looked around and found for her a little nursery school run by

64

missionaries for the children of farmers. She enjoyed it so much that when she returned to Tokyo she missed her playmates and begged to be allowed to go to kindergarten. They found a kindergarten that was suitable and took her for her examination to enter in the new term in the spring. In Japan even babies take examinations to enter educational institutions. When she was told that she had passed the examination, she exclaimed joyfully, "Then I can go to kindergarten tomorrow!"

Her mother told her that the days would grow cold and winter would come, and snow. Then the snow would melt and the trees and flowers would begin to bud. Cherry blossoms would come out, and there would be dandelions in the grass. *Then* she could go to kindergarten.

The next day, playing in the palace garden, she found a dandelion in bloom and came running to her mother with it clutched tight in her fist. "Now I can go to kindergarten!" As Princess Michiko hesitated, wondering how to soften the blow, the little girl understood and said sadly, "One dandelion is not enough?"

After dinner there was a reception to which all my old friends among the ladies-in-waiting and chamberlains were invited. The son of the man who was Grand Chamberlain in 1946 is now in charge of Prince Hiro. Most of the chamberlains whom I knew best have left to go into business or to head up schools and colleges, but they had come back for the party, and it was good to see them. Mr. Yasuhide Toda, who was the youngest and most boyish, is still in attendance on the Crown Prince; the hair at his temples is white now, but he still has a glint of boyish humor in his eye.

As I think about the Crown Prince and his family, I wish that he had more scope for his abilities. There is no provision in the new constitution for the abdication of an Emperor, and this is no doubt what is keeping the present Emperor from stepping down in favor of his son. If the Emperor consulted his own wishes, I am sure he would prefer to be relieved of his duties and be free to pursue his scientific interests. He is a marine biologist of real standing, with several books to his credit. The Crown Prince at thirty-nine is ready for responsibility and would bring fresh ideas to the ancient throne. Two years ago Akira Hashimoto, his classmate and friend at the Peers School, said of him to me, "He is a strong man; he has a pure heart; he dares to make innovations."

The earthquake yesterday was more severe than I had realized. The bullet trains were stopped for about twenty minutes; electricity went off in some places. Kayo Akiyama's thirteen-year-old niece cried out, "I don't want to die now!" and four friends of Tomi Koizumi's, knowing her fear of earthquakes, telephoned her afterward to inquire if she was all right.

Friday, December 8

It rained all night and into the morning, but then it cleared. What glorious weather I have been having!

Miss Hani sent her car to take me to Jiyu Gakuen—

Freedom School. Despite all the new building around its edges, the school itself is still beautiful, with its lawns and trees, its traditional low buildings and air of serenity and freedom.

We went first to Mrs. Hani's room, which her daughter keeps as a memorial and the shrine of a saint. I wonder how the Japanese have time to do the things they do: fresh flowers every day before a photograph, and appropriate meditations—with a school to run and visitors to entertain.

As we sat there in this little museum, surrounded by photographs and mementos, Miss Hani told me again the story of the school during the war. Two men from the Education Ministry came to labor with Mrs. Hani about the subversive name of her school, Freedom School. They suggested that she call it the Hani School or Minamisawa School, for the suburb in which it is located. They did not threaten her, Miss Hani wanted to make clear; they were not rude; but they stayed all day and they tried very hard to convince her. She told them that the name came from the Gospel of St. John, "You shall know the truth and the truth shall make you free." "We understand," they said, "but the military don't. Please change it." Mrs. Hani said, "If the name has to be changed, we will close the school." They went away defeated. Graduates who went into the army (as privates, not officers) and girls who worked in a war factory were so outstanding that the army began to inquire about the school that had produced them. The army did not want it closed.

Even so, because of its innovative methods, the school could not have the academic standing that made it possible for its graduates to enter Tokyo (then the Imperial) University, and without graduation from that elite institution no government position was open to them. But boys continued to come to Jiyu Gakuen anyhow, and after the war the government was delighted to have so modern and enlightened a school to show off to the Occupation and visiting Westerners.

She was a remarkable and an original woman, Mrs. Hani, and I am glad that I knew her. She was Japan's first woman journalist, she started the first women's magazine, *Fujin No Tomo* (The Woman's Friend), and with the proceeds from that opened her remarkable school, where the students, boys and girls, do the work of the school, study the usual academic subjects, and learn, every one of them, to play a musical instrument and lead an orchestra.

I remember taking Miss Hani once to visit Germantown Friends School, and sitting in Stanley Yarnall's office while he told her of the things that G. F. S. girls and boys did. "Do you have anything like that in your school?" he asked her kindly. "Do the children help in anything?" "They do *everything*," chirped Miss Hani in her high, girlish voice, "except pay the teachers' salaries!" And they do.

We went the rounds of Freedom School: a gym class where fifth-year boys and girls marched, ran, jumped, kicked, lay on their backs and made *kanji* in the air with their legs, all in unison and without pausing, for twenty minutes; a singing class; mothers preparing lunch for the primary school; an art class out of doors doing pen-and-ink sketches of trees; classes in pottery and weaving; and the handsome new library, which was silent as a tomb.

Mrs. Watari from *Fujin No Tomo* joined us, and we had lunch in the girls' dining room, a good lunch prepared by students, to which ten boys are invited each day. Coeducation is limited here; the boys have their own dining room. The afternoon ended with an impromptu concert put on for my benefit: primary-school children singing folk songs in parts; high-school boys singing the "Pilgrim's Chorus"; high-school girls singing Britten's "Festival of Carols," all well done, disciplined, and joyous.

The JAL pilot killed in the dreadful crash of a JAL plane in Moscow last week was a Jiyu Gakuen graduate, about thirty-five years old and much loved. Miss Hani told me that his young wife went to Moscow and brought his ashes back. Twenty or thirty other pilots stood in line with taut faces and saluted as she passed before them bearing the urn with his pilot's cap on top. There was a memorial service for him at the school.

At six Tadao Yamamoto, one of my best students, very handsome and tall, came for me with his car and took me to the Kasumigaseki Building, forty-three stories high and the first skyscraper to have been built in Tokyo. There are more now and, I think, even higher. The Crown Prince and Princess Michiko were already there at the restaurant on one of the upper floors, and about fifteen of my former students and their wives. It was a buffet supper, with champagne, and all very warm and lively. The wives, some in kimono and some in Western dress, clustered together, and the men hung together, but Princess Michiko and I circulated. Akira Hashimoto had just returned from the Philippines, where he and other newspapermen had been hunting for Onoda, the Japanese straggler from the war in the jungle, and had failed to find him. He feels the generation gap in his work, he told me: new young men are coming along, without manners, and crowding his generation, who are now thirty-nine and forty.

Hiroshi Kusakari, who sells Guinness beer in Japan, was master of ceremonies and a very charming host. The Crown Prince, who does not often have a chance to see his old classmates and who was obviously enjoying them, still had time to talk to me.

We had our pictures taken, we sang "Auld Lang Syne" in Japanese—which always makes me cry—and then Tadao indicated that he was ready to take me back to International House. "Aren't you going first?" I asked Princess Michiko. "We'll see you off," she said.

Tadao drove me back and came in to talk. He is running the educational program of N.H.K., national television. He skis, plays golf, goes to concerts and art shows, plays the piano. He will not marry again, he said, because he is always thinking of his wife, who committed suicide a few years ago. He asked me about the generation gap in America and about the state of religion. He is still at sea, he told me, about the purpose of life.

Saturday, December 9

I have been aware of two fears here, the fear of another great earthquake like the one in 1923 and the fear of returning militarism. Yoshiko told me the other day on the way to visit Keisen School and Junior College that a teacher in the Peers School, which her son attends—and where once a week from 1946 to 1950 I taught—teaches the constitution in a negative way, condemning its war renunciation clause and democratic principles, advocating a return to the rightist point of view. She said, too, that the postwar history textbooks were being constantly revised in order to present Japan's part in World War II in a more successful and respectable light. Today at lunch I asked Shio Sakanishi if she thought such fears were widely felt.

It is more than twenty years since I met Miss Sakanishi, but I have heard so much about her from her friends in the United States in the interval that I feel as if, instead of losing touch with her, I had actually come to know her better. At seventy-two she is a brilliant and interesting woman with whom one can communicate immediately.

Wearing a brown suit with a brown fur shoulder cape and neat brown pumps, she looked very smart and young when she came to take me to lunch at Ten Jin, a tempura restaurant on the Ginza. She has discontinued her very successful interview program on national TV, but she is still a police commissioner well into her second term and in the top place. There are only five on the Police Commission, which is a nonpolitical post and carries great responsibility and prestige. She is looking forward to revisiting the United States when her term ends. Since three of the five commissioners were out of the country several years ago when Ambassador Reischauer was stabbed, there are now strict rules forbidding any police commissioner to leave the country while he or she is in office.

She asked me eagerly about Mayna Goodchild, her close friend from prewar days in Washington when she was head of the Oriental Department in the Library of Congress. She was glad, too, to have the latest volume of May Sarton's poems, which I had brought her. May had stayed with her when she visited Japan several years ago, and some of the poems in the book about Japan were written in Miss Sakanishi's house in Oiso.

She told me that great earthquakes come at about fifty-year intervals and that the 1923 one was preceded by a number of smaller quakes such as those we have been having recently. (Three more since the one five days ago.) People are apprehensive. Yes, there is also a fear of returning militarism and the police state, but she thought more fear that the present prosperity would not last. The economic growth of which the outside world is so aware is evident in the public sector but has not got down to the lives of ordinary people. It seems to the Japanese that the United States in its present economic policy is picking on a small country. We are asking them to reduce their imports into the United States so as not to compete with our manufactures.

She told me that Princess Michiko is immensely popular with the Japanese people. It was difficult for her, at first, to be thrust, a commoner, into the age-old pride and formality of the imperial court and its jealousies, but she has learned to ignore them and in the process has matured, supported and helped by the Crown Prince's loyalty and devotion. She does a great deal of good in the country, notably in her work for retarded children, who have for so long been hidden away as objects of shame. Her popularity has been a help to the Imperial Family as a whole, and the government is shifting some of the Emperor's responsibilities onto the shoulders of the Crown Prince. I am delighted to hear this.

Sunday, December 10

My last Sunday here. The day was cloudy, and for the first time there was smog so thick that my sinuses were clogged.

It has been a full day: Friends Meeting, lunch with the Bryn Mawr group, a visit from one of my former students with his wife and two attractive children; dinner with the Matsumuras in their modern, expensive, elegant, and terribly small apartment. From their eighth-floor windows they have a beautiful view over the roofs and lights of the city on one side, and on the other of Tokyo Tower blinking its lights above the trees of the College of the Sacred Heart and the gardens of a temple.

I have been with Tané and Yukio many times in the past three months, both at home and here. When shall I

73

see them again? There will be a continent and an ocean between us, and we are all getting older.

New York. Monday, December 11

So here I am, in bed in a motel near Kennedy Airport, having left Tokyo at 6:30 p.m. Monday and having arrived in New York at 6:15 p.m. Monday. The actual time in the air was a little more than twelve hours, with something more than an hour in the VIP sitting room at Anchorage, where I dropped a glove. JAL found it and sent a wire and I will receive it by mail—their last gesture to me as a cherished traveler. There was a JAL man here at Kennedy to help me through customs and see me into a taxi, but he could not prevent the taxi driver from fixing his meter so that it did not register and then overcharging me.

It was a good flight. Very few people were on the plane; I imagine that some had canceled because of the crash last month. There were moments of great beauty: the midnight-blue sky and a huge, bright planet growing smaller and fainter as the light warmed on the horizon; the red sun slipping into view below the bank of clouds that I had thought was the horizon; the snow-covered mountains, the white, frozen river looping over a rocky gray landscape, and after hours of a cloud floor the slice of moon brilliant in the sky. At last, far below, I saw the lights of New York sparkling green and silver and gold and red in countless geometric designs.

The final day in Tokyo was a happy one. I had two hours in the library in the morning—interrupted by half a dozen telephone calls—poring over the wonderful book of the Genji scrolls, of which I had a glimpse in Kyoto. Princess Takako, very smart in her black-and-white suit and black turtleneck jersey, came to have lunch with me, driving her own car by herself. She has completely freed herself from her imperial shackles. When Their Majesties were in London last year, she went there on her own, quite by herself, stayed in the Sherlock Holmes Hotel on Baker Street, and observed them from a distance. She is great fun.

The Matsumuras came to take me to the airport, where the Chrysanthemum Room was reserved for the friends who came to see me off.

So the Japan trip is over, and I am wondering what was its meaning. Was it all just a glorious good time? I enjoyed the Conference immensely, but I made no contribution to it. I did not have time to work in the library at International House as I intended, and I do not see how I could write the book about Japanese women that I thought of. I feel fairly battered by the generosity of the Japanese and deeply touched by the warmth and faithfulness of my friends. I saw almost all the Imperial Family, including Princess Chichibu. I saw three of the Inoues, that dear family who worked for me in my house during those four years in Japan. I visited schools that I loved—International Christian University, Keisen, Jiyu Gakuen. I was with Tané in her married home. I saw Taki Fujita and Shio Sakanishi and Tatsuo Takaki and Tomi Koizumi, four inspiring cases of old age lived fully and gracefully. A rich, rich time, and, I think, somehow, the last time.

Alden Park. *Tuesday, December 12*

The time adjustment is about the same, whichever direction I go. I wake up at 3:30 a.m.

The weather today was cold and rainy—like the day I left, but colder. Fran had to spend some time getting the night's ice off her windshield before she could come to 30th Street Station to meet me.

We went to the Meditation Group this afternoon. For thirty-four years this little group of women has been meeting two afternoons a month to meditate together. Of the twelve or so who come regularly, five of us have been part of it from the beginning.

After all the miles and hours in the air, the brilliant and unaccustomed sights, the deep emotional stirrings, it was good to sit in this quiet, familiar circle and let the layers of silence settle and soothe.

Thursday, December 14

A little sunshine this morning and then clouds. Everyone says the weather for the last month has been rainy and dreary, while it was so lovely in Japan. Fran has gone to spend Christmas with her son and his family in Washington.

I went to the Christmas luncheon of the Germantown Study Class and to the Bryn Mawr Board meeting as Trustee Emerita.

Friday, December 15

Six appeals in today's mail, all long envelopes stuffed full.

To most of these organizations I have already contributed, and all of them have sent me several appeals already this year. This is a great waste of paper, stamps, and time.

Saturday, December 16

Fran Stokes at lunch in the low-ceilinged restaurant, not hearing me and hating to ask me to repeat; "Deaf people talk all the time, because that's the only way we know what's being said."

Living at Foulkeways, she regularly visits her sister-in-law and others in the infirmary there, and daily sees her older friends sick and confused and feeble. She said she was going to spend Christmas with her grandchildren. "It will be noisy—everybody talking and nobody listening—but I've had so much geriatrics I'll be glad to have some pediatrics for a change." Then she added quickly, "But I'm not complaining. I like it there. And when I get too much I just retire into my own place and read."

She is very gallant and gay and loving; she utters no nostalgic moans for the rich and absorbing life that she had before her distinguished husband* died suddenly two years ago, the trips they took together, the laughter they shared. Is there such a thing as a naturally happy disposition, I wonder, or can it be won by prayer and self-control?

Wednesday, December 27

For the first time in more than a week I have seen the sun.

---

* Dr. Joseph Stokes, Jr., was a well-known pediatrician and one of the developers of gamma globulin; he was the recipient of the Medal of Freedom and many other awards and medals.

It rose crimson and promptly disappeared, but then it came out again as I was driving along the Schuylkill after having delivered Ruth Miller to the railroad station on her way back to her job at the J. I. C. U. Foundation in New York. What a difference a little sunshine makes! It brought out the muted violet and russet in the bare trees and turned the sky a pale ice-blue, where all before had been gray and black. Rufus Jones wrote once, "The weather molds me like wax." But he was a young man then, and he learned better as he grew older. I am too old to be so much affected by it. But I do wish yesterday had been sunny for Ruth, who was here for such a short time.

Christmas is over and all the presents are given and received and opened; all the pretty and thoughtful, the useless and trivial things have found a place somewhere. More and more I welcome the consumable: food, calendars, soap, wine. With Kendal ahead I have to reduce my possessions, not add to them.

The Christmas Eve, Christmas breakfast and dinner that I had with Elizabeth and Jeanie and Jeanie's daughter, Mary Lou, were warm and comfortable and happy. There was good talk, good food, some music, time for reading, a walk in the gray mist, a comfortable bed for sleeping, the ease of being with old and understanding friends with whom I can talk without weighing words.

For how many years now have Elizabeth McKie and Jeanie Buck—and Violet, when she was here—spent Christmas together? It has been such a good friendship ever since Chapel Hill days, first Elizabeth and her father, and then Elizabeth and Jeanie when Jeanie retired from teaching at Kalamazoo and came to Swarthmore. Elizabeth and Jeanie are planning to sell their house and move to Kendal when it opens—another inducement to me to go there. Yesterday Ruth came, and I took her to see the hummingbird exhibit at the Zoo. Outside, the scene was dreary: bare brown earth, dark clouds, a few people in drab raincoats. The monorail was closed for the season; refreshment stands were bleak; unfinished buildings with gaping windows were surrounded by a clutter of machines and piles of sand. Then, without transition, we entered a bright, warm tropical garden with little streams, rocks, hanging vines, red-blossomed mimosa, orange or white anthurium, padded-looking leaves of all sorts. And everywhere, darting through it, flying before our noses as we walked the narrow board path, were bright hummingbirds of all sizes and colors, some with long forked tails, some with red crests and blue backs, some with white on their heads, some that looked black till they turned and flashed a brilliant, metallic peacock blue. Sitting on a branch, walking the ferny floor, hovering at a feeder, whizzing past our eyes faster than thought, making small noises that still were larger than their tiny selves.

Out of the dazzle and the color we emerged into the rain, drove home along the lead-colored river to the warm, bright apartment, and spent the evening talking about the problems and successes of the International Christian University in Japan.

Sunday, December 31. Rain

New Year's Eve, the last night of 1972. It has been a disappointing year on the whole: the war in Vietnam continued with appalling bombing by the United States of Laos and Cambodia as well as North Vietnam, while the American public was quieted by the withdrawal of many American soldiers and the promise of peace. McGovern suffered a humiliating defeat and Nixon was re-elected by so large a majority that he seems to consider himself all-powerful. During the last two weeks, with Congress recessed, he has ordered the saturation bombing of Hanoi and Haiphong, and this after having declared just before the election that peace was on the point of being achieved. I think the man is insane—and the fear of being in the hands of an insane ruler is a very real one.

But on the personal side, there was my trip to Japan, I had a book published and got on with a new one. *The Taken Girl* came out on August 28, my twenty-third book. It has had good reviews and some enthusiastic letters from both friends and strangers. I am happy about it.

At Germantown Meeting today a mentally disturbed man, not a Friend, who has invaded one meeting after another shouting about peace, began to speak after a long absence. One of the problems peculiar to an unprogrammed meeting for worship is that anyone from outside may invade the meeting and take over what appears to be an unoccupied pulpit to set forth the particular bee that occupies his bonnet. This morning our unwelcome visitor began by saying fairly quietly that Friends have the reputation of being lovers of peace. As he spoke he walked up the center aisle and his voice rose to a shout. Now, he screamed, the Number One Quaker was bombing Hanoi. I could feel the shudder going through the meeting house, the indignation at having our silence so torn, the recognition that what he was saying was true, the physical and psychological cowering under the blasts of noise.

The Friend who sat on the facing bench at the head of the meeting came down the center aisle and tried quietly to coax him out. He resisted, shouting, "This is what happens when anyone tries to speak about peace!" Someone else joined the first Friend, and together they shoved the intruder to the door, where he took a last stand, yelling, "Shame! Shame! Killers!"

They got him out, and he could be heard shouting beyond the door. A young Friend went out and joined him, and the noise died away.

After a few minutes of silence, intense and searching, one of our wisest and most beloved members rose and told a story of a meeting for worship in Japan at which a member, having spoken amiss, apologized, saying that the water was pure even if the pipe through which it came was not. Someone at the back of the room spoke sympathetically of our disturber, charging that he had not been treated with either love or justice. The speaker was followed, after an interval, by a member of the American Friends Service Committee staff, who spoke movingly and raised the quality of experience in the meeting.

"The word 'shame' rings through our meeting-

81

house—shame for all the wrong things done by our society, the right things not done; shame for our personal failures—but also resolution to do better."

These were not his exact words, but the ideas were these. The first Friend, who had taken the lead in getting the visitor out—and had been publicly "eldered" for it—rose and quoted the thirteenth chapter of First Corinthians, adding with great humility that he was sorry for having acted without love. And so our apparently shattered meeting ended on high notes of unity and repentance.

Now, near midnight, on the verge of a new year, I am thinking about what I, personally, repent of. Not loving enough, being self-centered, self-righteous, lazy, self-indulgent? All these—and more.

Monday, January 1, 1973

A mild, sunny day. I watched the Mummers' Parade on TV for a while. This would be a good time to have a color set. Those fantastic costumes must have been brilliant. It is one of the few really indigenous folk festivals that we have in this country, and it is a colorful and original and energetic one. The Mummers march for ten miles, the length of Broad Street, "strutting" in a sort of dance, diagonally back and forth, so that another five miles must be added to the distance, carrying all the way those high, heavy headdresses and the frames of their vast costumes. Some of the marchers have children with them, too, small boys taking part in their fathers' tradition. And then the music! The succession of string bands. And the individual entrants: a man-sized rooster, Jonah and the whale, a dragon with a sixty-foot tail. I was eight or nine when I saw my first Mummers' Parade, on an icy day, from the steps of the Union League. It is better on television, even without color.

Now for the new year. I can settle in again to my book on Whittier, which I had to put aside for the Matsumuras and for Helen. I am glad that it is a biography and not a novel; it will suffer less from the interruption. This is my real life, writing. Other events and forces have been climactic, have shaken me to the depths and rebuilt me, marriage especially and my Japanese experience, but day in, day out, year in, year out, writing is the basis of my life. And deep winter is a good time for writing.

Tuesday, January 9

Still there is no peace. Kissinger was received icily in Paris. When I think of what we are doing in Vietnam, of the way the United States is supporting oppressive governments in other countries, of the billions Congress appropriates without question for military spending, while the school lunch program is dropped, of the millions spent on restoring Philadelphia's Society Hill section while parts of North Philadelphia are *rotting*, of the state of our prisons, of the fact that we can't get a decent gun-control law and people are killed every day—when I think of these and many similar things, I burn with helpless rage.

And then the craven, comforting thought seeps into my

mind: I am seventy and before too long I shall be out of it all.

Sunday, January 14

Will I know how to keep silent as the years go on? The Quaker Discussion Group met at B's apartment tonight for the first of a series of six meetings. Her mother was there, a small edition of B herself, with all the angles sharpened. She was introduced to us all, and while we drank coffee she was the center of the conversation. When the discussion of Quaker journals began, she became restless and understandably bored, but instead of slipping out quietly, she said in a rather loud, rasping voice, "If you all will excuse me, I think I will go to bed."

We assured her that she was excused and waited for her to depart. But having got the floor, she kept it—told us how she slept, how much she liked to read in bed, what she read, and then, with a leap to another subject, all about the hours she spent rolling bandages for the lepers. Her daughter and son-in-law were so admirably patient that I assumed that she was a temporary visitor, not a permanent resident. Having talked till she ran down, she finally left, and we took up the business of the evening.

Is it possible to accept the fact that one is not necessarily interesting to younger people, that silence is not only graceful but more desirable than speech? After she left I was the oldest one present. Did I talk too much? I had pertinent historical information that the others didn't. In the past I have been more likely to err by not speaking up than by saying too much, but this could change without my realizing it. Should the old, like the very young, speak only when spoken to?

Wednesday, January 17

Whittier wrote at eighty, "I do not believe it possible . . . to be sinless." It would seem that if anyone had led a blameless life, he had. But so did all the saints lament their sins. I think I know what they meant.

After one has passed the stage of committing the grosser sins and even of being tempted by them—temptation having been removed by age or lack of opportunity—then the hidden spiritual sins come flocking: pride, envy, jealousy, anger, all forms of concealed unlovingness, and that sin considered today to be the top one of all, hypocrisy.

As hypocrisy is the major sin in the eyes of today's young and not so young, so openness and honesty are the chief virtues. The thirty-five-year-old Irish poet Brendan Keneely defines goodness as "openness and vulnerability, a willingness to walk the dangerous line where one can be wounded or foolish, yet gathering experience unto oneself." It is an interesting and a fresh way of looking at goodness, and yet it seems to me self-centered, a definition of vulnerability itself, rather than of goodness, which surely is born of love, and love is not so concerned with its own experience.

Whittier elsewhere was disturbed by the gap between what he wrote and what he was. This is a different form of Yeats's dilemma:

The intellect of man is forced to choose
Perfection of the life or of the work.

Whittier would not have hesitated over the choice; with him the life always came first. The trouble was that he felt that his statements of aspiration outran his performance.

Yeats chose the work—"So get you gone, von Hugel, but with blessings on your head." And so have other great writers. The new biographies, which are so appallingly frank and detailed, give scandalous pictures of the lives: the selfishness and bad temper of Robert Frost, the promiscuousness of Katherine Mansfield, the homosexual affairs of others. I am reading Quentin Bell's biography of Virginia Woolf. He was her nephew, and I must say it offends me to see him discoursing so explicitly on his aunt's sexuality, or lack of it, and his mother's extramarital affairs. I wish he had said more about his aunt's books and the writing of them, the sources of themes and characters and so on. There's no doubt that the book is interesting, but is a writer justified in invading another's privacy in order to entertain the general reader? Ten years ago I wrote a novel about John Donne, using my imagination to fill in the gaps in the known facts. I had the feeling at the time that the lapse of three hundred years put him in the public domain, so to speak, but should I have done this, really?

Conversely, there is in the air an implication that a blameless life is a passionless one and that the work is weaker because of this essential lack in the writer. It is also arguable that understanding of the life makes possible a better understanding of the work.

But fundamentally I do believe that the work is the artist's contribution to the world and that his life is his own. I see little value in exposing Frost's night fears, for instance. His poems speak for themselves. Cassandra Austen has been reviled for burning Jane's more revealing letters and saving only those that showed the lighter side of her nature. But the novels stand on their own feet. What matter whom Jane loved or how she really felt about the Napoleonic wars? How fortunate for us—and for him—that Shakespeare's plays are produced by generation after generation and Shakespeare himself is a mystery!

Wednesday, January 24

A happy awakening this morning. I had been dreaming about Mother. Nothing very special; we three were in a hotel and wanted to leave earlier than we had planned. Violet and I set Mother to arranging it with the proprietor because we felt that he would be softened by her charm. The impression of her beauty and wit was still with me when I awoke.

My next thought, also a happy one, was that the peace agreement in the Vietnam war will be signed, at last, in a few days.

After that I was hungry for breakfast and enjoyed my orange juice, coffee, boiled egg, and toast. Breakfast is the best meal of the day, anyhow, and then to have it facing the drama of a winter sunrise! First the golden cloud islands in a sky of forget-me-not blue, the gold brightening by the minute, and then suddenly the glimpse of fiery red among the trees. The sun rose quickly and in moments was a huge blazing globe that I could no longer look at.

I am thinking of those two little girls whom I saw at Ogunquit in Maine four or five years ago, coming up from the wide deserted beach at twilight, slapping their sides with their hands and singing joyously:

> *If you're happy and you know it*
> *Slap your sides!*
> *If you're happy and you know it*
> *You really ought to show it!*
> *If you're happy and you know it*
> *Slap your sides!*

Monday, January 29

To Kendal to have lunch with Barbara Jones. She has already moved into one of the sample apartments, one of those with a den—with fireplace—as well as living room, bedroom, bath, and kitchen. It also has a terrace opening off the living room, and space for a small garden.

Mary Hoxie Jones and her friend Tina were there, too, and we were all very merry over luncheon. Until the Center Building is finished, Barbara gets all her meals in her own kitchen, a nice one with a window and space enough for her gateleg table. When the place is really going, everyone will take at least one meal a day in the central dining room.

Kendal looks like a good thing.

A letter came yesterday from Allan Hunter about his wife, Elizabeth, who died recently. I remember well my first meeting with her twenty-five years ago. She was slender and fair and steady. The letter was a moving tribute to her. Apparently she kept up a running mental prayer throughout the day for love and—this I like especially—a sense of humor about herself: a very endearing prayer.

Gerald Heard (who was a great friend of the Hunters) said once in my hearing that a sense of humor was the modern equivalent of the medieval virtue of humility. That was at Pendle Hill* in the summer of 1938 when I was head resident. There were sixty students scattered over Pendle Hill and neighboring houses, and the summer school lasted for six weeks. Anna Brinton was the head of the nonacademic side of it, and I was her assistant. The cook and I planned the meals together, and I went in my small car and bought the food and brought it back. Twenty-five pounds of meat one hot day almost made a vegetarian of me. I also made the beds for unexpected visitors at 10 p.m., burned the Kotex, oversaw the work schedules, and filled in gaps wherever they occurred. I have never worked so hard in my life, but it was a growing time for me, or, better, what Rufus Jones used to call a spiritual equinox.

Every day after lunch I used to go to my room over the pantry and lie down for half an hour, with my feet higher

* The Quaker center for study and meditation, in Wallingford, Pennsylvania.

than my head, for I had a fallen kidney at that time. Below me the lunch crew washed the dishes. One of them was a Chinese girl, studying in the United States, who had been brought up in a Christian school in China where she was taught gospel songs. One of them was "Till We Meet Again," but with a difference. At the end of the hymn her voice, which was rich and lovely, soared up in a final line, "Lord, make me more loving, lo-o-oving," and fell on "Till we meet again."

I had no idea what happened to that girl. I don't even remember her name. She is probably a grandmother by now, if she is still alive. But her voice soars through my mind from time to time as I go about my daily things and now and then "step home," as William Penn said, and inwardly ask for more love. I should like, too, to have a sense of humor about myself.

This is my forty-fourth wedding anniversary, a brisk, cold, sunny winter day. I saw the sun rise behind the trees. Forty-four years—almost forty of them without Morgan. Perhaps we should not recognize each other if we met now. I am not the same person that I was when Morgan died. But I am more like Morgan's wife now than I am like the green girl he married on January 31, 1929. Without the four years and eight months that we had together I should be only a stunted growth, a bud that never really unfolded. Morgan released me. Our love and the time we had together were the greatest things in my life.

90

Saturday, February 3

Stopped for gas at the station which last week was robbed of forty tires, in spite of police dogs chained there all night. Last night, they told me, a man had driven up, bought nine dollars' worth of gas, and driven off without paying for it.

"A black man," said the owner of the station sourly.

The young black who worked there, who had a sweet, merry face, said ruefully, "That's all I needed."

Can they ever escape from their color?

Tuesday, February 6

On the *Today* show a young woman of thirty-two talked about the book she had written about old people, *Nobody Ever Died of Old Age*. She had taken jobs in a great many places where old people are living, in order to get material for her book. She is very sorry for old people and for the way they are stuck off in retirement homes and nursing homes. The title was chosen to attract attention, she said, but it is true that people don't die of old age; they die of specific diseases. She has great admiration for old people and for their courage in the face of death; only the old face death every day, and she herself is afraid of death.

At seventy I don't face death every day. It is a fact of life, of course, a part of life as natural as birth. It is there, ahead, but I don't think about it every day. It floats into my mind from time to time, awakened by a reference in a book, the death or serious illness of a friend, or just suddenly appearing out of nothing.

I don't fear death, but I do fear a protracted and painful dying, and I have signed a "living will" directing my doctor not to keep me alive "by artificial means or 'heroic measures.' "

Thursday, February 8

Less than a week now and I shall be off for Ossabaw Island, Georgia, to be a resident in the foundation for artists, musicians, and writers created by Eleanor and Clifford West. It is a venture into the unknown. Years ago I went to Sea Island, which is at the southern end of a string of islands off the Georgia coast. Ossabaw is the northernmost one. I have never met the Wests, and I've no idea who else will be there. Still, from what I have heard at second hand, it sounds like heaven.

Two speeches lie between here and there, and a long drive through February's uncertain weather.

Baltimore. Wednesday, February 14

Off this morning by car for Baltimore, first stop on the way to Ossabaw. The morning was lovely, a chilly spring day in February, with pale sunshine and delicate shadows. When I swung into I-95, though, I saw a cloud bank in the west, high and solid and definite as a range of mountains. Halfway to Washington the air turned raw and cold, and soon sleet was rattling against the windshield.

The rain was pouring down in Baltimore, and I got lost

in a dreary part of the city, looking for the school in which I was scheduled to speak. But even after a lot of circling around and left turns against traffic, I was early. I am always early. It's pathological. The counselor of libraries, Alice Rusk, was my hostess, a very attractive and knowledgeable woman. We had good talk over lunch, and afterward the auditorium was full of school librarians; the response was good, the questions fun.

Annis Duff was there and brought me home with her to spend the night in her enchanting house, which is full of mementos and trophies of her happy marriage and her children, her life as a writer and an editor. Through the windows were glimpses of her garden—the East Garden, the West Garden, the Wild Place, the Pool Garden, the Water Meadows, all in a little more than an acre.

Williamsburg. Thursday, February 15

I got off a little after ten in a thin, watery sunshine which soon retreated into clouds. For a long time the flat landscape was gray, dun and sand-colored, but from Port Royal on the Rappahannock east to Yorktown the woods had color: the green of pines, dull russet of lingering oak leaves, muted gold of occasional beeches. There were two fields of cattle, but in the rest of the more than fifty miles it was an empty country. Here and there were houses but almost no people. I saw one woman, one man, on foot, four beagle hounds off on some obviously satisfactory project of their own. Otherwise there was no one in the fields, no one coming out of a house. I passed one shabby little unpainted wooden store with a large sign advertising "guns" and "sorghum."

When I reached the Colonial Highway from Yorktown to Williamsburg, the sun came out. There were ducks—mostly ruddy ducks—in the York River, and in Williamsburg a few yellow tulips. You can't take a car now into the old part of Williamsburg, and so I parked and walked for a while. The newness has at last worn off the restorations; it all looked a little shabby and *triste*—and much more convincing. But the outskirts are horrible—motels, restaurants, shopping centers, cars, signs.

There is no trace here of the big snowstorm that paralyzed the South last week.

New Bern, North Carolina. Friday, February 16

Sunny, mild, and windy. The James River, which is really an estuary at Jamestown, was high and muddy and so rough that the ferryboat had to make several tries at the dock before it succeeded in getting in.

I am amazed at the emptiness of this country. In a day's driving I could count on the fingers of one hand the people I saw walking along the road. There were no local buses at all. Much of the time there was not even another car in sight. Practically no birds and few animals: an occasional herd of cows, two fields with pigs; a few dogs, a cat or two, one pony, one old horse.

Suffolk seemed—on the map—a good place to get lunch, for it stood at the junction of several roads and the name was printed in bold letters. It turned out to be the "largest peanut center in the world" and was jammed with cars, possibly peanut growers in town to do business. Where they ate I do not know, for I saw no restaurants at all, and the country beyond was devoid even of hamburger joints. Then suddenly at the bridge over the Chowan River was a sign, Chowan River Inn, and on the left an attractive building on stilts over the water.

It turned out to be a rather sophisticated restaurant, run by the wife of the head of one of the industrial plants that appear to abound along the river. The clientele seemed equally divided between surprised tourists like me and young executives in suits and ties. The waitresses wore gold-colored pants to match the tablecloths, and one of the young men addressed one of them as "Miss Nancy." Not just Nancy—*Miss* Nancy. How southern! How nice!

There was no life on the river—no birds, no boats, just a few smokestacks in the distance.

New Bern was jammed with lines of cars full of people going home. I am established in the Holiday Inn on a point where the Trent and Neuse rivers come together. I've seen the outside of the Tryon Palace (reconstruction), and the lawns and trees within its high brick wall, but I was too late to go in.

I have come nearly five hundred miles, and what a number of splendid rivers I have crossed since I left home: Schuylkill, Susquehanna, Potomac, Rappahannock, York, James, Chowan, Pamlico, Roanoke, Neuse! I am making the trip in a very leisurely way, having allowed time to be overtaken by bad weather. (High piles of dirty snow left

95

from last week's storm still stand in New Bern's parking lots.) I am much more cautious at seventy than I was at thirty, more aware of all the possibilities. The days—three of them now—have been solitary but not lonely, the country flat and almost monochrome in its winter coloring but not dull. There is much to see and to think about.

I love this country, not just this flat, coastal bit, but all of the country that we call, incorrectly, America. There are things about it that make me sick and angry: the hideous, vulgar strips outside the cities, all alike with their signs and crude colors; the commercialism and the violence of our television; the mounting corruption of our government; our unconquered and so often unconscious racism; the squalor and vice of our slums (not a nice word but a better one than ghettos); the control that the Pentagon and the makers of munitions exert over our lives; the greed of the unions and the industrialists alike; the rape of the land and the proliferation of highway systems. All these I hate, but the country itself, the ordinary, hard-working, generous people and the ideals we still hold: these I love, and our rivers, fields, woods, mountains, beaches, our villages (the prettiest are in New England), our old Pennsylvania stone farmhouses and big trees.

Charleston, South Carolina. Saturday, February 17

Myrtle Beach, South Carolina, was a horror of motels and hotels and inns and apartment houses with every kind of decorative and eye-catching motif: Aztec, Amerindian,

Hawaiian, Spanish, Olde English, early American, modern, gaudy in color and plastered with huge signs. Most of them professed to be open all year, and there were many parked cars but no people to be seen. A ghost town. One man walked on the beach, which is still wide, firm, and white.

When Morgan and I were here in 1930, there was a shabby frame hotel at one end and a pleasant, rather simple golf club at the other, and in between was the lonely beach and the sand dunes overgrown with myrtle.

Coming away from it, feeling jangled and puzzled, I arrived before long at Brookgreen Gardens, and as I drove in the long, beautiful driveway lined with trees and pine-cone-strewn grass, I felt physically soothed and gentled. The grace of the different gardens, the great live-oak trees with a little—not too much—moss, the pools, the pieces of sculpture, the river down below, the birds everywhere: it was all so perfect and so quiet. There were daffodils, looking a little chilly and small, and red camellias turned brown by the frost.

There was rather more sculpture than I can take an interest in all at one time, but it was all lovely, and traditional. I remember especially a young *Diana* by Anna Wyatt Huntingdon, who with her husband created the place; young *Ben Franklin* by Tait MacKenzie, my father's friend; many endearing animals by Paul Manship; and Sylvia Judson's *Girl with a Squirrel*. On the grass beside the river were some dumpy brown birds with long bills poking into the mud at the edge of the water—Virginia rails. The woman in the information office told me that the head of the South Carolina Ornithological Society was there yesterday to see them. He said that the river had risen and forced the birds up on the grass, that only once in a lifetime would one see such a sight.

Savannah. Sunday, February 18

Charleston in the Sunday morning quiet was lovely. All the region below Broad Street is just as it was when I was there in 1935, preparing to write *Beppy Marlowe*, except that the Miles Brewton House, where I spent those six weeks, is not open to the public now and the Fort Sumter Hotel has been rebuilt. The sun was out and the air fresh. It is past the middle of February, but there was not even a narcissus in bloom. The occasional people whom I saw—a white-haired man bringing home the Sunday paper, a slender, middle-aged woman with a cairn terrier—looked like such *nice* people. WASPS. (Snob.)

As I type this I am forced to think about the acronym WASP. I know that to many Americans today WASP is a pejorative term. I intend no disrespect to those two "nice" people whom I saw; I am only jeering at myself for being so pleased to see them, looking so much like people from that golden age before World War I—false gold, of course, but we thought it was real. My papa—pronounced with the accent on the second syllable—used to go out on Sunday morning, before the rest of us were up, to get the newspaper; he would leave the comics, then called funny papers, behind so that my young eyes and taste should not be sullied by their vulgarity. (I read them next day at my friend's house.) These people whom I saw today were of Anglo-Saxon or perhaps French lineage; they might have been Roman Catholic but were probably Protestant, possibly members of St. Michael's Church nearby. They had, to me, the nostalgic charm of a disappearing species.

Now I am at the DeSoto Hilton, in Savannah, where I am to be met tomorrow morning and taken to Ossabaw Island. There is nothing left of the old Desoto but the name. When Morgan and I stopped here on our honeymoon, it seemed fabulously grand to me. I remember a palm court in the center of it, and in the morning a black waiter rushing to us with small cups of coffee to fortify us for the labor of deciding on fried ham and grits for breakfast.

I got here early and took a walk down Bull Street through the different squares, just as Morgan and I did. Tomorrow my adventure begins. Usually when I am approaching a new place, a new situation, I have some mental picture of it beforehand, some fantasies, but this time I am blank. I cannot imagine Ossabaw or its people. But I am happy about it.

Ossabaw Island. Monday, February 19

So here I am, after a fifteen-mile ride in a car to the private dock and a forty-five-minute ride in a motor launch to the island. My car is parked at the dock, and there were two young men to unload and carry the electric typewriter, the metal file cases, and the box of books that comprise most of my luggage. I feel as if I were in a play, an old-fashioned one, possibly by Barrie in one of his supernatural moods.

The house is large and beautiful in the Spanish style of 1924, with spacious, old-fashioned rooms. It looks out not on the open ocean but on the stretch of water between the island and the mainland. It is surrounded by enormous live-oak trees liberally hung with moss. Underneath them is a sort of aqueous green light, and the sun comes through in flakes and lozenges. I've heard a pileated woodpecker, a towhee, and a Carolina wren; jays and robins are everywhere; a hermit thrush ran under a camellia bush, and a kinglet moved among its leaves.

I have been given a large room and elegant bath, all a little dark, for everything is painted delft blue—hence the "Blue Room." There is a sturdy card table for my typewriter, and also a small, neat blue table with a floral design on the drawer. French windows lead out onto the terrace.

Breakfast is at eight-thirty; lunch is sandwiches and soup ready in the kitchen whenever you want it; dinner is at seven. Once a week the boat goes to the mainland and you can go with it for errands or just for a change if you wish. There are no shops on the island, no radios (unless individuals have them in their rooms), no television. I can see that there will be no obstacles to work.

I met the resident group at dinner, twelve of us about halfway down the sides of the long, candlelit table. Eleanor West, a vital, even a glowing, person, sat at the

100

head and kept the conversation moving. (Clifford West will come later.) We are: a journalist, a university professor, a young composer, the wife of an Anglican clergyman—who is writing a first novel—two published novelists, two young artists. Charles and Anne Wood are the managers.

I asked about walks. There are definite, named trails, and you must stay on them for safety reasons. All the poisonous snakes that exist in the United States, except one or two rare rattlers, flourish on the island, as well as wild cattle, wild pigs, deer, and donkeys. My neighbor in the Yellow Room will show me one of the trails tomorrow afternoon.

Wednesday, February 21

We have visitors with us, a couple from Medford, New Jersey, who showed us last night their color slides of the Pine Barrens. What amazing hidden beauty in those miles of sand, pines, and scrub oak that look so dull when you whiz through them on the highway!

At breakfast this morning Queenie, the cook, honored the Everetts by coming into the dining room and singing "Lord, take my hand" in her deep, rich voice. As she sang she walked around the table, taking each one's hand in turn. A strange and moving performance out of a lost past.

Thursday, February 22

It is interesting to be working on Whittier on this southern island, which is so different from his New England landscape. He never saw any of these islands, yet he imagined them so vividly. There were once four plantations here, on which indigo, long-staple cotton, and rice were grown. As I see the now abandoned fields and the swamps where once the slaves toiled, the small tabby houses (actually very good architecturally by modern standards) where they lived, I keep remembering Whittier's "Farewell of a Virginia Slave Mother to her Daughters Sold into Southern Bondage":

> *Gone, gone;—sold and gone*
> *To the rice-swamp dank and lone,*
> *Where the slave-whip ceaseless swings,*
> *Where the noisome insect stings,*
> *Where the fever demon strews*
> *Poison with the falling dews,*
> *Where the sickly sunbeams glare*
> *Through the hot and misty air; . . .*

In summer, I am told, flies, mosquitoes, and other insects make life all but unendurable, even though the house is screened, and in spite of whirring electric fans the brooding heat steams day and night.

Isaiah, our bearded young artist, is painting a large picture beside the path to the crescent of beach called the Little Beach. The canvas lies flat on the grass, and we see it as we pass. There is a spot of light in the center with a little clutch of white marbles or eggs, surrounded by colors—green, purple, blue, cerise, in dabs on dabs. He has left it out all night and is waiting to see what nature will

102

add to it and what changes will occur in it. "A cow may step on it," he said. Whatever the accident may be, he appears to welcome the participation of nature.

Friday, February 23

How to write of enchanted days? The chapters of my book flow in an uninterrupted atmosphere where everybody is at work and my neighbor's concentration reinforces my own. In the afternoons I walk under the live oaks, looking out over the water to low wooded islands. Evenings are spent sitting around an enormous fire, talking, listening to the tapes of our young composer's music, or looking at the movies that the Wests have made of the island and its life.

Indians have been here, and pirates, Jesuit missionaries from Spain, Oglethorpe's Scots adventurers, the plantation people with their slaves. Then came northern sportsmen, bringing the first prefabricated house in the world from the Centennial Exhibition in Philadelphia for their clubhouse, and finally the cultivated, appreciative Chicago millionaires, with their Rolls Royces, servants, children, governesses, tutors, ponies and pony carts, giving house parties, inviting the Savannah ladies to tea. And after them the writers and artists, musicians, ecologists, archaeologists, biologists, who come to savor, enjoy, study, but cannot stem the tide of progress. The island is threatened by the clutching hands of developers, of city planners, and even of state foresters, who would like to give the people of Georgia access to beaches, camping sites, and recreational areas. Gallant Eleanor is like a modern Canute bidding the waves roll back. And everywhere the ghosts are waiting.

Sunday, February 25

Six of us went off in the jeep to the beach, nine miles away, through avenues of live oaks that made me think of an English park, different as the vegetation is. The flocks of pigs and cows have kept the undergrowth down, so that there is the same sort of vista through spaced trees. Now and then there was a black pond, now and then an opening up of golden marshland, and at last the low dunes and the open sea with a mild ripple of surf. But the foam on the breakers and the foam washed up on the beach was not white; it was yellow. Even here, away from houses, miles from the city, the waters of the sea are polluted.

The beach was beautiful, wide and white and hard. There were dunes and twisted, bare, gnarled remains of trees long ago destroyed by salt and sand and wind but dramatically lovely in their fantastic shapes and contrasting dark color. A brown pelican came flying along just above the surface of the waves; a common tern dived; a piping plover and a semipalmated plover, small and lonely, scurried along the sand.

The group scattered, and we went on our separate walks. The immensity of sea and sky and beach swallowed us up and left each of us alone until hunger drove us back to the jeep. We ate our sandwiches and drank our coffee in a hollow of the dunes, out of the sharp wind. We were visited by Durkee, a Sicilian burro imported some years ago by the Wests, followed at a distance by his five dejected-looking wives. When the sky clouded over we came home.

Tuesday, February 27

I have no idea what is happening in the world outside. There is just the beauty here, the tunnels of sun-flecked shade through the live oaks, the sun on the water, the pile of pages growing steadily on my desk, the talk at the dinner table and around the fire.

Rosalind has gone, and Evelyn is in the Yellow Room next to me. She is the author of a beautiful and sensitive book about Africa, and an exquisite person. We have had some walks together.

We sign up on the blackboard in the weaving room, giving the time of our leaving, the trail we are taking, the time we expect to return. When we come back, we rub it all out. Anne Wood checks it regularly, and if any have been away much longer than indicated, a search party is sent out. This is not a tame island; there are real dangers. It is still too chilly for snakes, but there are other wild creatures; there is the possibility of getting lost and bewildered among the trees and creeks, or foundering in a bog, the chance of slipping and spraining an ankle, or of encountering, as Eleanor once did, moonshiners from the mainland. She was on horseback; she rode away quietly, and that night two or three of the men on the place, armed with guns, went out and surprised and frightened away the moonshiners.

Even the mansion is not without its terrors. People hear

footsteps at night; they start out of sleep in cold terror. Kaye, who has had my room in other years, awoke once feeling herself surrounded by an evil presence and was paralyzed by fear.

"But don't let them drive you out," she said. "I used to keep a Bible or a copy of the Bhagavad-Gita by my bed and pray, 'Deliver me from evil!' "

A man who had my room awoke on his first night there in the clutch of a fear so intense that he refused to sleep in that room again.

Others have heard screams and shots and maniacal laughter. Eleanor and her husband one night clung to each other for half an hour in such terror that they could not even go to see if their small son was all right.

Eleanor's theory is that the house is like a fairy tale, on an island hung with moss and magic, separated from ordinary life by the miles of sea; that the mind goes back to childhood when fairy tales were real, and that hidden and submerged dreams and fears come to the surface again.

I wonder how I should feel if anything strange happened to me. I rather welcome the idea, though I very much doubt its possibility; I am too skeptical about the whole thing.

Saturday, March 3

I walked on the Little Beach late in the afternoon. It is only an arm of the bay that washes up here with the tiniest of ripples through a stretch of reeds, but the sand is fine and hard. It was marked today by tiny round holes, each one surrounded by a fine scattering of sand in patterns like snowflakes. Old palmettos and old pines had fallen from the crumbling banks and lay across the beach—stark skeletons. The colors were subtle—grays, taupes, faint blue, faint green, black. Loneliness was the main impression. No fiddler crab came out of his hole; there was not a bird to be seen, until finally a killdeer flew crying over the shallow water.

Sunday, March 4

A perfect day—deep blue sky, soft air, little wind. We spent most of it on South End Beach.

Off to the east I saw a pale gray strip along the horizon that looked like a low range of hills, but flat on top, and I said to myself, "If this were Maine that would be a fog bank." Soon wisps of gray began to blow in scarves along the beach. I thought at first it was sand but soon saw that it was mist. It came and went. I walked along the beach toward a sand spit where there were two hundred or more gulls and terns, sandpipers and willets, and one great blue heron with the longest neck I have ever seen on a bird.

The rest of our group had vanished, and I was alone on the wide, beautiful, empty beach. Hardly any waves were coming in; the tide was very low. There was a shallow gully and on the edge of it hard, wet, ribbed sand. The sun was warm.

And then suddenly the fog was there, all around me. The sea disappeared. The trees on the shore turned to pale shapes. It was not a wet, clinging fog like a New England one; it was soft, blowing, caressing, gentle. It stayed for a while and then it moved on. The beach came back, the sea was blue, there were again a horizon and a deep blue sky. The trees were solid, with other trees marching behind them. I went back to the group.

On the way home in the station wagon we saw an otter dash across the road and into a pond. Deer down the corridor of the trees raised their white flags and vanished. At the egret pond we got out and walked to the edge for a better view of the far side, where white egrets looked as if they had been pasted on the dark trees. On a bare bush sat an anhinga, or water turkey—a strange and exciting bird.

Sometimes during the day I thought about being old. I am older than anyone else in the group. I don't feel old, and I don't feel sure of myself—not sure, that is, that what I say will be interesting to these vital, younger people. Yet I know that they, too, are not really as sure as they seem. They—most of them—are testing their lives against one another. Mine is now irrelevant.

Good health and enough money—not a great deal, but enough—are important elements in a happy old age, but not all of it by any means. A naturally happy disposition is an invaluable asset. Congenial, interesting children and grandchildren must be a glorious enrichment. Curiosity, wonder, pleasure in the companionship of one's own thoughts: these too are good.

It is something of a shock to me to realize that I have reached the point where there is not much chance that I will succeed in making any notable changes or improvements in my personality or character. Somehow I have assumed that this was an endless possibility and that in time I should be able to decide exactly what I want mine to be and get it formed that way. Now I know that I am firmly set and not subject to alteration. Oh, I hope to go on growing, but the growth will have to be along the old lines. Just a little more of the same—and then the effort to hold the line and not deteriorate. Acceptance—an ideal but not always a practice—is now a necessity. I think of the song from *Porgy and Bess*:

> *No matter what you say*
> *Ah still suits me.*

A sensible attitude, and the wise young man in the play adopted it in good time.

Monday, March 5

Last night I dreamed that a voice said to me, "You must scream as loud as you can. Scream. Scream louder. Scream again." There was no personality connected with the voice, only a colorless disembodied voice and a sense of compulsion. I screamed—and woke standing by the window, on the far side of the room, waiting for an answer. When no answer came, I looked out of the window into the courtyard, where a light was burning. I don't remember that a light has burned there other nights, and it looked strange on the dark bushes. I realized slowly that I had been dreaming, hoped earnestly that I had not waked anyone, and, feeling terribly silly, went back to bed. As I slipped into sleep I had a distinct feeling that, whatever the voice had been, it was laughing at me.

In the morning I felt oddly drained and exhausted and wished that I did not have to get up. Nobody spoke at breakfast of having heard anything in the night, and I did not raise the question till afterward. Kaye's room is over mine, and I asked her if she had heard me. She said that she had dreamed she was collecting screams in a silver cart and woke to hear someone crying, "Aye-aye-aye."

If this had happened last week when we were all talking about the supernatural manifestations in this house, I would have supposed myself suggested into it. I have occasionally walked in my sleep before this, but never, so far as I know, created any sort of disturbance. Screams in nightmares usually emerge in small, strangulated squeals. I feel humiliated, as if I had yielded to some form of hysteria.

Tuesday, March 6

Evelyn in the Yellow Room next door also heard me the night before last. She said there were five screams. At first she thought someone was having a nightmare, then she thought that they were not like the tight squeals of a nightmare but that they sounded as if someone were being stabbed. She waited, uneasy, but heard nothing more. Pat, down the hall, also heard, but this came to me through a third person; I did not hear from her directly. She did not open her window last night, lest she again be disturbed. Odd that none of the three who heard me thought of getting up and coming to see if I was in any trouble.

In the afternoon I went off for a long walk by myself, to the end of Cane Point Island Trail and back. Part of the way was through a deep, old forest. Here there was total silence—no bird calling, no rustling of palmettos, no wind in the live oaks. It was like the Sleeping Beauty story, when everything slept under a spell. In some ways this island *is* under a spell. Later I saw a boar, quite a big one; farther along there was a doe, and when I came to the river, five black skimmers were flying in formation, and eight cormorants on a sand spit were drying their wings and looking like heraldic birds.

As I walked I thought a good deal about that episode in the night. I remembered the long walks that I used to take that winter after the accident which so swiftly and finally took Morgan from me. I felt then that I had a scream pent up inside me ready to burst out, and I felt too that if I let it go I would be all scream; there would be nothing left. If on this island one regresses to unresolved episodes of an earlier time, then it might be that I finally released that long-ago scream. But what about the mocking laughter? As if a malicious voice were saying, "Well, you asked for it, didn't you? You thought you were so skeptical."

At any rate, I have no intention of moving out of the Blue Room. While I was undressing last night, I had a few fears that I might again wake people up or that I might have some even more disturbing experience, but by the time I got into bed, remembering some poems and prayers, I was in a peaceful, even euphoric frame of mind.

111

This afternoon I went, along with Eleanor, Anne, the two artists, the professor and the Shorter College students, on a marsh walk led by Dr. Philip Greer, the leader of the Shorter College group. We drove to South End, where the students were camping in blue and orange and green nylon tents. Dr. Greer discoursed—very interestingly—on marshland, the most valuable land there is, he says, and the source of twenty per cent of the oxygen we breathe.

The marsh grass, spartina, was much shorter than I expected, the muck deeper and wetter and slipperier. We saw periwinkles clinging to the grass and fiddler crabs scurrying over the muck, little piles of raccoon dung, a herd of black pigs in the distance. The proper way to go through marsh is to put your toes down first, to step on green if you can, and not to stay long on any one spot. I wore sneakers and socks and my denim pants rolled up. Most of the rest had boots. One of our writers wore his gray suit trousers and black oxfords and academic rubbers, one of which he lost in the muck. I found it and pulled it out for him. Anne had nice wool pants stuffed in her boots, and a beautiful golden raincoat. Somehow she got mud up to her knees and spattered all over the coat. It was so slippery that for a time I thought I was going to measure my length in it, and I dreaded the ignominy. But I managed to keep my balance.

When the walk was over, I washed most of the mud off my sneakers under a hydrant and joined the circle around the campfire, where Dr. Greer was expounding his theory about the evolution of primates. He said that he and Sir Alistair Hardy had developed the same theory independently of each other. I was interested to encounter Sir Alistair Hardy again, that retired professor of science at Oxford whom I last met in the *Manchester Guardian Weekly*, where he was encouraging its readers to send him accounts of their mystical experiences for a study he was making. Some apes left the trees, Dr. Greer said, and took to the marshes. There they had to walk upright, develop sensitive fingers for groping for food, develop solid, short-toed feet, downward-pointing nostrils, and hairless bodies like other aquatic mammals. This was in the period before their brains began to grow. While we sat around the fire, listening, three white pelicans flew up and down the creek in front of us, and behind us a bluebird perched on a fence post. Coming home, we stopped at the heronry and saw that the number of egrets and herons had increased to sixty.

We were told that one of the Shorter College students had seen a four-foot rattlesnake. Obviously the snakes have now begun to emerge from their winter lethargy, and we have been cautioned to look where we step.

After dinner we saw Evelyn's exquisite color slides of Africa. I wore my new long skirt, which I had bought in Savannah on Friday—green and orange printed with fishes and butterflies—to counterbalance the image of my floundering through the marsh mud in pants and sneakers, and everyone commented on it approvingly.

Thursday, March 8

The first all-day rain since I have been here. Without my walk, I got a lot done at the typewriter.

In the evening about thirty Shorter College students came in to hear a talk by Eleanor on Ossabaw Island. When I came into the living room, they were all sitting down, in the chairs, on the window seats, the long sofa, the floor. I found a place on the hearthstone. The young people near me, on the hearth and in the facing chairs and sofa, were very friendly. They included me in their conversation, but not one of them, boy or girl, got up and offered me a chair. Obviously such an idea did not occur to them—nor, in fact, did it occur to me till afterward.

Perhaps I should be flattered, on the principle that, having seen my floundering in the marsh yesterday, they did not think of me as an aged woman needing special treatment. But the point that sticks in my mind is this: manners as such have completely disappeared. In my day we would all have hopped to our feet automatically when an older woman came into the room, even one not anywhere near seventy, and she would have had her choice of seats.

Sunday, March 11

Not actually raining today but still no sunshine. I walked in the grounds. Far out on the water I saw hundreds of ducks, but they were too far away for one to tell what kind they were.

Under the live oaks there was suddenly a great commo-

114

tion—jays flying wildly and screaming, robins darting about. A hawk, I thought. Then I heard the unmistakable, high, two-syllabled cry and saw a broad, swift swoop of wings and short fan-shaped barred tail. A chestnut-breasted bird, larger than a crow, perched on an open limb high above me and cried again. There was another swoop from above the trees, and a second bird, the male, came and mounted the first.

It lasted only a moment, and then the male red-shouldered hawk was gone. The female evidently wanted more, for she moved from bough to bough, calling, but he did not come again. The jays were gone now, but a Carolina chickadee high in the top leaves was singing.

What an experience! To see the beautiful birds mating, not preying on smaller birds. Not that I hold that against them; they have to eat too.

Tuesday, March 13

Today was so beautiful that I could not stay indoors. The azaleas are in bloom, flaming in the green aisles of the live oaks; there are violets in the grass and redbud against the sky. I walked along the edge of the lawn, looking across the marsh, where a green veil is beginning to show, thinking of the doomed beauty of this island. How long before it will be taken over for a state park, with places for parking cars, trash cans at which no one aims successfully, picnic tables, grills for cooking hamburgers, notices—all the dreary results of sharing beauty with the masses?

I took *Snow-Bound* down on the little beach to reread.

One of the few idylls in American poetry, it is perfect in its genre. "The sun that brief December day . . ." It is made up of contrasts: between Whittier's then and now, boyhood and age, night and day, the cold outside and the warmth within, life and death, love and fear, fire and snow, the simple life about the hearth and the mysteries evoked by the tales they told. Reading it here on this southern beach on a warm spring day, I added yet another contrast.

In the afternoon I walked the Cave Patch Island Trail again—my favorite walk, about six miles. As I went silently through the woods, making no rustle with my feet, suddenly I heard two explosive cracks, like a car backfiring or shots. Then I saw smoke rising through the trees and a black man moving in the distance.

I thought, if this were a gothic novel, the heroine would at once start off to investigate, would be seized from behind, blindfolded, gagged, and carried to a hidden place. I thought, he is probably doing just what he has been told to do—and I have been told not to go off the trail. So I went on, over the causeway, where the fiddler crabs were busy in the sand, to the end of the island and the river. The tide was high and there were no waders, just two black ducks swimming. So I came back, and when I reached the place where I had heard the shots, I went off the trail to see what was there.

No black man, no smoke. There were some old broken iron things lying about; there was a pit with ashes in it. Obviously it was the dump.

116

The days are warm now, 75 today, 80 yesterday, sunny with a little breeze. The dogwood is in bloom.

Everybody is gone except the Woods and Eleanor, Kaye, the novelist, and Lin, the journalist, and me. Soon we too shall be gone and the place will rest over Easter. It is quite different now from the active, lively, stimulating atmosphere when all the rooms are full, but it is restful and relaxed and very pleasant in its different way. A dinner party every night is fun but strenuous; this is intimate.

I have done all that I can do on my book without recourse to a library. I have loosened up a bit within myself; being for nearly four weeks with lively-minded people younger than I has been good for me. I think of age from time to time; I recognize that I am now out of the mainstream, and I am content. Long walks every day have been satisfying. And the beauty of the island!

I wonder sometimes about the retirement community at Kendal, which must be moving steadily toward its opening next fall. How much would it depress me to be surrounded by aging and dying people? How much would the pressure of the community bother me? But Chester County is beautiful. There would be walks there, too, and people whose lives have been interesting and significant. I should still have my car, my work, my summers in New Hampshire. My life would go on much as it does now, except that I should be surrounded by friends.

Violet's birthday. She would have been ninety if she had lived. It seems much more than three years since she died—and of course it is, for she was not really herself for five and a half years before that, ill and paralyzed as she was. I miss her very much—her companionship and her enchanting humor.

Yesterday I saw a mourning cloak butterfly among the azaleas on the patio, dark-winged with a border of yellow and black spots. I saw a pileated woodpecker at the top of a bare tree against the sky, a dramatically beautiful bird with its fiery red crest, long bill, long neck, black body with white under its wings.

I wish I knew how to describe the sound of boat-tailed grackles in flight. Pigeons creak. Small birds rustle. A boattail has a fuller, heavier sound, rather like the emptying of a bottle of liquid. What a contrast to the silent, mothlike flight of an owl.

Last night Kaye heard loud, troubled sighs and the tapping of high heels on a bare floor.

Saturday, March 17

It poured in the night and blew wildly. All the furniture on the patio overturned and slid and banged. But in the morning the sun was out, the sky a deep, clear blue, the air cool and dry.

I said good-by to Eleanor and Kaye and Lin. My suitcases and typewriter and the files were loaded into the jeep. The launch was waiting at the dock. The passage to the mainland was windy and rough and slow but beautiful. My car, waiting patiently at the mainland dock, started right up. I said good-by to Anne and Charles Wood, who were going off to Charleston for a breather before the next batch of people comes.

All day as I spun along the smooth, straight superhighways toward Southern Pines, I thought about Ossabaw and what the experience there had meant.

I have seen fiddler crabs, hundreds of them, sitting by their holes, waving their big pink claws to attract a mate. I have seen red-shouldered hawks mating. I have seen a black anhinga among the white egrets at the herony. I have walked and skidded and squelched ankle-deep in the marsh and learned why marshland is so important to our very existence. I have sat at the long table in the formal dining room night after night with stimulating and sometimes brilliant people and afterward sat drinking coffee before a fireplace so large that veritable yule logs burned in it. I have walked on a broad, hard beach where for fifteen miles there was no human being except those of our own small group. I have walked alone through deep woods and marsh across an island to a river where five skimmers flew in formation. I have outfaced a boar and a cow with a calf, have seen deer running among the trees and a raccoon sniffing at the ground. I have screamed in my sleep, loud enough to rouse the house, and have awakened standing by a window waiting for an answer and getting only a half-discerned laugh. And I have had hour after uninterrupted hour to work on my book. Twenty-six days of it.

The wind was strong all day; sometimes it seemed to push the car over the edge of the road. It caused a succession of dust storms so blinding that I could see nothing but the white line along the edge of the road. It seemed as if all the topsoil of Georgia, South Carolina, and North Carolina were in the air.

I thought of what bacteriologist René Dubos has written about "humanized nature." Much of the country through which I came today was dull, scrubby woodland, though touched with green and brightened by the occasional crimson of red maple blossoms. But where the land had been cultivated it had beauty: plowed fields, fenced or hedged; cattle, horses, barns, solid houses surrounded by trees at the end of long lanes. It was comforting to realize that here at any rate man had made the land more beautiful, not less.

In North Carolina I saw again the scarlet clay soil blazing in the late-afternoon sun. And oh, the blue, blue sky of North Carolina!

Southern Pines, North Carolina.
Sunday, March 18

The Penick Memorial Home (Episcopal) is an attractive place surrounded by long-leaf pines, blossoming shrubs, and grass. It is a one-story building with big windows, several competently decorated lounges, a chapel, a library (minimal), a recreation room, dining room, and a nursing-home wing. I went there to see my old friend Evelyn Brooks, but before I ever got to her I was caught in the reception room by a smartly dressed old lady who sat there like a spider waiting for someone to come by. She told me all about her arthritis and the treatments she was getting.

Evelyn is in the nursing-home section, but she is up and dressed and will soon be promoted to the residential side. She has kept her keen mind and her interest in world affairs, social problems, and movements; she desperately needed someone to tell her concerns and views to, as well as someone to talk to about her husband and her son, about ways of meeting sorrow, about memories, so many of which we shared, all the way back to the days in Chapel Hill when Lee and Morgan played tennis together, before we were married. It was such a good friendship: Lee and Evelyn and Morgan and I; then Lee and Evelyn and I; now Evelyn and I. A good deal of the day—except when we went to lunch and dinner—Evelyn lay down on her bed, but she did not want me to leave; she wanted to go on talking.

I left her to rest for a while and went to see Billie G., who also, to my surprise, was there. I haven't seen her for years, though she, too, was a good friend in North Carolina. Billie has always had spectacular illnesses, from which she has made determined recoveries. She now gets dizzy spells and falls, and when she falls she breaks something—a pelvis, a hip, an arm, a shoulder. She is in bed now with a broken hip and amazingly cheerful. She wanted to talk about her Irish qualities of resilience, of fight, of humor, about her apartment, her collection of Chinese porcelains, about her husband, Felix, who died a number of years ago, about her daughter and her incomparable granddaughter.

Now, back in my motel, I am thinking about the day, especially about Evelyn, who is so dear. All three of those whom I met, each so different from the others, had one thing in common: they needed desperately to talk. This is the real loneliness of old age—to be surrounded by people and yet not to have anyone to hear and respond. For myself I found the day strangely tiring. My heart was torn for Evelyn, and the things we talked about stirred my own memories and emotions. Then, too, I was thinking: this is a place for old people. Is this the noose I should put my head into at Kendal? Am I considering going into a kind of prison that I might stay out of for another ten years? Should I be surrounded at Kendal by people like that well-dressed, well-groomed old bird who buttonholes strangers to talk about her ailments?

Chapel Hill. Monday, March 19

This dear village where I spent the happiest years of my life (except for that last year that Morgan and I had in New York) has now spread over much of its surrounding woodland and is looped about with concrete highways that swoop over and under concrete bridges.

I am spending the night with Chesley and H. G. Baity. Their house on Mason's Farm Road, so stamped with their various interests and travels, stands on its hill surrounded by trees and overlooking a scene that is still mostly forest. They spend winters here and summers in their other house

122

in the French Alps. Years of service in the World Health Organization (H. G.) and the Literacy Movement (Chesley) in India and Africa lie behind them. Chesley is a Ph.D. in Anthropology, a writer and poet.

Before dinner H. G. went off to celebrate a colleague's seventy-fifth birthday. Three old friends—Adeline, Ruth, and Gladys—came in for dinner and we talked. We're not what we were, to look at, but what fun we had, flinging out ideas like tennis balls, tossing them back, examining them, commenting, questioning, disagreeing, assenting, qualifying! No gossip, no symptoms. And Gladys was still beautiful, her hair snow-white and well coifed, her eyes a clear blue, her jawline taut, her feet and ankles elegantly slender and fashionably shod.

Chesley, it seems, is a very great swell in the new science of astro-archaeology or archeo-astronomy. She has written a scholarly paper termed important by other pundits, and has just given a seminar that was called inspiring and first-rate. She is also deeply involved in parapsychology, ESP, and psychic phenomena. She teaches a course at the university on African art. She runs her house and takes care of a brilliant and somewhat turbulent husband of seventy-eight.

After the others had left, she and I talked on about religion. She told me that she had been drawn to the local meeting for worship by the Quaker contribution to social concerns and by Quaker mysticism, but she was disappointed. The silence at the meeting was short. Friends arose and held forth on Vietnam and nonviolent resistance

123

and what to do about the blacks. She said she agreed with it all and would have been glad to discuss it on a Wednesday evening, but that was not what she went to Meeting on Sunday morning for; she went for spiritual resources and enlightenment. She thought that people could change the world only if they were spiritually enlightened themselves. (An interesting modern echo of what William Penn said in 1691 of a band of young Quakers known as the First Publishers of Truth: "They were changed men themselves before they went about to change others.")

"I'd rather go and jump up and down with the Episcopalians," she concluded. "At least there is an element of worship there."

Many churches today are divided right down the middle on exactly this issue: does the church exist to provide spiritual inspiration or to change the social system? Perhaps Quaker meetings have more difficulty because every member is potentially a minister and can air his opinions unrestrained, since "eldering" has gone out of fashion. And yet a truly "gathered meeting," when the silence is deep and the spirit moves on the waters, is an experience of worship worth waiting for.

Tuesday, March 20

Chapel Hill was lovely this morning with redbud and daffodils blooming everywhere. I drove along North Street past the little house that Morgan and I built forty-three years ago. It stands among its trees (oaks, elms, cedars) gray-shingled with white trim, with an air of elegance, tiny though it is. All the other small houses built at the same time look shabby and tacky. It was pain to see it—and joy. Those two golden young people who lived there for three years belonged in another age, and perhaps to a fairy tale.

> *Fear no more the heat o' th' sun*
> *Nor the furious winter's rages;*
> *Thou thy worldly task hast done,*
> *Home art gone and ta'en thy wages.*
> *Golden lads and girls all must,*
> *Like chimney-sweepers, come to dust.*

These, I think, are some of the most beautiful lines ever written—and all with the simple words that everyone may use, but so fitted to the thought and the sound and to one another that together they take on a beauty and mystery far beyond their separate qualities.

She was young, Imogen, and actually not dead, only preserved by a potion until it was safe for her to live. But Arviragus and Guiderius, her brothers, thought that she was dead and said those perfect words over her as they strewed flowers on her body.

> *Thou thy worldly task hast done,*
> *Home art gone and ta'en thy wages*

expresses my fundamental conviction about death—and life. We each have some earthly task to do, and when it is done, we go home. When someone dies swiftly, of a heart attack, perhaps, full of years and honors, it is obvious that

125

his time has come, his task done. But what of those who die young, like Morgan in full stride, his Ph.D. within his grasp? Or those who like Violet suffer year after year of strokes, living on, yet not really alive, to eighty-five or more?

The task, I think, is not an obvious one, not visible to the outward eye even of love. It must be some inner act of growth, some hidden contract to be met, some ripening to be accomplished. "Men must endure/their going hence," says Edgar in *King Lear*, "even as their coming hither;/ Ripeness is all." Some ripen young; some take a long time to it.

And how can I be so sure of this, without believing in an anthropomorphic god or a bookkeeper in heaven? Only because I know—I *know*—that there is meaning in the universe, not chaos, and that love is at the heart of it.

Tuesday, March 27

A sharp letter has come from the controller of Alden Park. He says that all my rent checks have been coming in after the tenth of the month, and he threatens a surcharge.

I go back over my checkbook stubs for the past six months and find the checks dated 10/2, 11/4, 12/1, 1/5, 2/3, and 3/5. The March bill, which must be sent in with the check to get credit, did not reach me in Ossabaw until the fifth. Mail was sometimes slow in leaving the island; it might possibly have reached the office after the tenth. The others must all have been there well before the tenth.

126

The flood of rage that I feel surprises me. This letter is annoying but trivial. Why do I respond so vehemently? I think it must be the child in me reacting to injustice on the part of authority. I realized long before reading the popular book *I'm OK—You're OK* that there is a child within me that from time to time emerges and cries out to be recognized and comforted. I remember the time when Violet had her first broken hip and the day nurse failed to show up one morning. I tried to be an efficient substitute, coping with bedpan and bath and sandbags and traction, but I was inexpert and Violet was miserable and I felt overwhelmed. Suddenly I had an intense pain in my back. I remember saying to the child within me, "Yes, I know. You've just had more than you can take. But wait a little while. When Vi takes her nap, you can lie down, too, with a hot pad at your back, and then you will feel better." And, actually, I did.

There is no use being ashamed of this persistent child or denying its presence. It must be recognized, its need accepted, perhaps met, perhaps only acknowledged with some amusement.

Coming home from Judy Rubel's this afternoon, I was sitting in my car at the corner of Walnut Lane and Wissahickon Avenue, waiting for the red light to turn green, when a car smashed into me from behind. It was driven by a young girl, who was very apologetic. The trunk and one light are damaged. It could have been a lot worse.

On the whole, though, not one of my best days.

Monday, April 2

There were two birthday dinners at Valley Green tonight. The small, old inn on the Wissahickon looked as it might have looked a hundred years ago, with a fire blazing on the hearth and candles on all the tables. At the head of one table sat a handsome small boy of eight, with a row of adoring adults on either side. He was full of aplomb when his cake came in. He wielded a large, sharp knife with skill, asking his guests if they would like a piece of a rose, of Happy, or of Birthday. He put two slices of the cake on a plate and left his table to offer them to a couple near him.

We were seven at the other table, with my friend Eleanore, who must be well into her fifties, in the center. When her cake came in—plain chocolate icing and three symbolic candles—there was a burst of surprised laughter from the rest of the room and then the boy's voice rang out:

"I didn't know anybody so old would have only *three* candles!"

But even before the shout went up, the small diplomat made a recovery. "I didn't know anybody *twenty* years old would have only three candles!"

I cannot imagine having been at his age anything but shy and speechless in my happiness. Children mature earlier today, but even so I think this child had an unusual awareness.

Tuesday, April 3

Back in my home routine again, at work from nine to

twelve-thirty. It is the solid basis of my life, the soil out of which other things spring. If I could steel myself not to answer the telephone when it rings, I should make better progress. Most of my friends are good about respecting the sacred hours, but there are people who don't know or who forget. And of course it just might be an editor—which is another matter altogether!

Poets met this afternoon at Elizabeth Yarnall's, perhaps the last time at her house, for she is going to Kendal this fall. How many years have we gathered on the first Tuesday in each month at Roumfort Farm to read our poems, sitting in a circle in her large dining room, with birds coming to the feeders outside the many-paned windows, where little blue trees march up the curtains.

Wednesday, April 11

The day before yesterday Howard Brinton died. He was eighty-nine, lame and blind, and he had for the last two or three years been a transparent shell through which the light shone. Up to the end he was dictating his articles on the early Friends, his mind clear and retentive, his spirit shining. More than anyone else, except possibly Rufus Jones, Howard Brinton has for me expressed the essence of Quakerism today. And as a person he was lovable, gentle, wise, humorous, clear-sighted. He had had a stroke a few days earlier and was in the hospital under oxygen; at the end his speech returned and his mind was clear. Yuki, his wife, was with him day and night. His death was a serene transition.

What makes one dying peaceful and another painful? I have been reading the last volume of Leon Edel's great biography of Henry James. "The Master" at seventy-three had a stroke. He had servants, nurses, a devoted secretary around him. His sister-in-law, his niece, and his nephew came from America to London to be with him and to take charge. It took him nearly three restless, uncomfortable, irritable months to die. During that time his mind was much occupied with that which had been the absorption of his life—writing. He dictated to his secretary letters to Napoleon and others, essays, many meaningless but beautifully worded paragraphs. On February 24, four days before the end, he spoke of having had a night of "horror and terror." Altogether it was a protracted and difficult dying.

Whittier died at eighty-four. He was staying with a friend and cousin, Sarah A. Gove, at her place, Elmfield, at Hampton Falls, New Hampshire. On September 3, 1892, he had a stroke. His much-loved niece, Elizabeth Pritchard, came from Portland to be with him. For the three days that he lived, he was full of acceptance—"It is all right. Everybody is so kind"—and of love. Over and over he said, "Love, love to all the world." On September 6, as the sun was rising, he died. It was a peaceful and beautiful dying, and brief.

Violet had two years of immobility and silence and apparently of unconsciousness after her last stroke, and then died alone in her room in the nursing home. I was not there. I could have been. I went to see her several times a week, but I did not know that the change was coming.

130

This I can hardly bear, even now, after more than three years. Even if she knew nothing, I would have sat beside her. I would have been there.

Teilhard de Chardin prayed for a "good end" and died swiftly of a heart attack. Two years or so ago I wrote such a prayer for myself.

O God our Father, spirit of the universe, I am old in years and in the sight of others, but I do not feel old within myself. I have hopes and purposes, things I wish to do before I die. A surging of life within me cries, "Not yet! Not yet!" more strongly than it did ten years ago, perhaps because the nearer approach of death arouses the defensive strength of the instinct to cling to life.

Help me to loosen, fiber by fiber, the instinctive strings that bind me to the life I know. Infuse me with Thy spirit so that it is Thee I turn to, not the old ropes of habit and thought. Make me poised and free, ready when the intimation comes to go forward eagerly and joyfully into the new phase of life that we call death.

Help me to bring my work each day to an orderly state so that it will not be a burden to those who must fold it up and put it away when I am gone. Keep me ever aware and ever prepared for the summons.

If pain comes before the end help me not to fear it or struggle against it but to welcome it as a hastening

131

of the process by which the strings that bind me to life are untied. Give me joy in awaiting the great change that comes after this life of many changes, let my self be merged in Thy Self as a candle's wavering light is caught up into the sun.

This prayer, like many others, is really addressed more to myself than to God. And I am not at all sure that by the time one has reached seventy one can do anything at all about the manner of one's dying. Whittier and Teilhard de Chardin and Howard Brinton had won their way of dying by their way of living over the years before.

Monday, April 16

"The Group" was here tonight, sixteen strong, and we discussed Transcendental Meditation and the fourteenth-century anonymous *The Cloud of Unknowing*. Douglas Steere was in especially good form and illumined the subject well.

It is a fine group. There are no young members now, though when it started thirty or so years ago, with seven or eight couples, they were all in early middle age. Now there are several widows and everybody is retired, from business, from teaching, from social work, except Don Rubel, who is still an active broker, and me, who still writes. And, of course, Douglas, who, though retired from his Haverford professorship, still travels about the world, lecturing and writing.

I wonder sometimes how long I can continue to write

things that will be readable and salable. For the present I have an audience of my own age and interests, but it will inevitably grow smaller, and publishing houses need larger and larger audiences in order to break even under today's conditions. I have been told that it is not worth while to publish an edition of 5000 copies nowadays, though once this was satisfactory to everybody. I write for myself and because I enjoy writing, but also I write to be read. To write without being read is rather like that book of Bishop Berkeley's that falls in an empty room and makes no sound because there is no one to hear it. And to be read I must be published. And how long will I have the freshness and vigor to go on writing? Sometimes, treasonably, the vagrant thought crosses my mind that it would be restful not to feel the compulsion to write every day. But no doubt I shall know when the time comes, when ideas give out, as they have not so far, when I cease to feel guilty if I am not writing.

In how many different ways this business of growing old comes at one! Days go by when I scarcely think of it, days full of the usual—or unusual—activities, and then the thought springs up: but I am seventy!

Wednesday, April 25

Spring is early this year. The dogwood is out, and lilacs and apple blossoms. The trunks of the sycamores are palely dappled with cream color, green, and lavender.

Emma Engle and a friend of hers came from Clarksboro bearing asparagus and lilacs. They are planning a trip to

Scotland, and I had a glorious time giving them brochures and advice.

Friday, April 27

An old-fashioned storm, what we used to call a north-easter, cold, with a driving rain and buffeting wind out of the northeast. I had to go to town to get an X-ray of my neck, which appears to have suffered a whiplash injury when my car was bumped at the traffic light. The shoppers' bus, which runs on a schedule, was twenty minutes late. It was cold waiting on the street corner, and my umbrella tugged in my hands, threatening every minute to turn inside out. I thought of the people who wait every day on street corners for buses in all weathers and in the dread of being late for their jobs, and I thought how fortunate I am. But at that moment I was very miserable and impatient.

At the doctor's establishment on the fifteenth floor I disposed of galoshes, raincoat, rain cap, umbrella, and all my clothes down to my waist, the hairpins in my hair and the bridges in my mouth, and was photographed over and over on a hard, cold, slippery table, in positions that hurt my neck. I then got dressed again, resumed all my paraphernalia, and went out into the rain and wind without having laid eyes on the doctor—only his secretary and the brisk, impersonal X-ray technician.

The streets were swept by gusts of wind and sheets of rain. On every corner huddled a score of drab-looking people waiting for a bus. Evidently the buses had retired for the day. I came home on the train, and when I got out at Chelten Avenue the skies opened afresh. In the block and a half between station and home I was soaked.

At Kendal all this sort of thing will be done on the place, in the medical center. Will I remember, when I am there, how it used to be, or will I take it all for granted?

Friday, May 4, 3:15 a.m.

I wonder why one's thoughts at 3 a.m. are so meager and dreary. One could lie and remember poetry, visualize past scenes of beauty, think of absent friends, plan books. But no, I wander in a dreary maze of trivialities and fears. In the morning, when it is time to get up, how different! Then my mind is full of interesting and exciting and beautiful ideas that should be pursued in leisure and comfort, right there where I am, in bed.

The X-ray showed up not only the whiplash injury but calcium on the carotid artery, and arthritis. I have a surgical collar, and I wear it in bed as well as throughout the day. It is an ugly thing but very helpful. I have made some silk covers for it out of a Japanese *furoshiki* with a plum blossom design.

Thursday, May 10

I have been spending a good deal of time going through files and possessions, weeding out in case I should move next fall. Yesterday I went through early journals and notebooks, which I really shouldn't like other eyes to see, yet which I might like to read again myself at least once.

135

Much of it is childish and occasionally self-pitying, but some of it has lovely memories that have grown dim. I found my JAL ticket in a correspondence folder.

Among the questionable things is the journal entry, made when I was thirty-one, about old ladies and their classification. The old ladies who surrounded me then were Aunt Emily, seventy-five; Cousin Emma, seventy-five, and Mother, just seventy-three, and actually they did not fit into any of the categories, except perhaps "bossy," for I was then very sensitive about bossiness. I wrote: "I think it quite probable that I shall be a batty old lady, supposing that I manage to avoid the other pitfalls." Then I expressed the hope that I should not live to be any of them. I continued: "I am sorry for old ladies. Failing faculties and failing looks must be a constant irritation to unfailing vanity. The answer to the riddle of life is so near—and the only thing that really interests them is the satisfying of their own whims, their own comforts, the obtaining of admiring audiences; they are like children in their demands, yet with the habit of authority of their prime still firm in them. One pities them, one loves and cherishes them, one can so rarely like them."

These are harsh words from arrogant youth—or early middle age, when one first becomes aware of age. But perhaps they are salutary for me now. What I did not at all perceive at that time was the effect of increasing physical deterioration. It is to the credit of my three old ladies that they did not burden me with accounts of their high blood pressure, failing sight, encroaching deafness. They must

136

have had a gallantry that I took for granted or did not see.

Today we are no longer old women. We are senior citizens, a euphemism I dislike as I dislike all the other evasions: health center for medical center, and all the rest. We have better doctors now and face having to live longer but not more healthily. We still want independence (satisfying our own whims), comforts, and an audience.

Back to my journal, where I went on to say: "I think perhaps there is no one trait quite so satisfying both to oneself and to the people around one as *joie de vivre*. An old lady who has a genuine joy in living is an old lady who draws people to her. She is sufficient to herself. She has something to give—a gift the more precious and the more endearing because it is quite unconscious." These, I think, are wise words and true. I did not go on to cite examples, but I believe, as I look back, that all three of my (perhaps) batty, fussy, and bossy old ladies had it.

Saturday, May 12

Just back from my walk. Buttercups are in the grass, even where it was mowed, which means that the mower has gone around them, like the tuft of flowers of Robert Frost. The magenta azaleas are gone, and the white ones are beautiful. Most of the trees are fully leafed, though the oaks are still in bud. The air was full of bird song: cardinals, ovenbirds, mocking birds, song sparrows, chestnut-sided warblers, robins, wrens, brown thrashers, and catbirds. Other warblers, too, which I did not recognize. Also a pheasant croaking in the Wissahickon woods.

I have a little more trouble seeing birds now, in spite of strong binoculars. Though Dr. Adler said my cataracts are slow-growing and my eyes have not changed enough to warrant new glasses, and though he said not to come back for a year, I do not see birds as well as I used to. So I think I shall take to trees. They are eminently visible and stand still to be examined. They have leaves, blossoms, and fruit that can be carried home to compare with pictures in a book. In winter their leafless shapes and varied bark offer points for identification as well as enjoyment. I brought home this morning leaf, flower, and seed of a mountain maple.

The Watergate horrors go on and on, spreading far beyond Watergate itself. An attorney general of the United States has been indicted for perjury, plus other charges, but perjury seems to me the lowest and most intolerable.

We are getting along badly without the Protestant Ethic. Truth, duty, honor, justice were ideals perhaps often betrayed, but at least they were ideals, and we measured ourselves by them. For a long time now I have been hearing people declare that hypocrisy is the worst sin, if not the only one, but I am not at all sure. "Hypocrisy is the tribute vice pays to virtue." If people used to pretend to be more honest, more chaste, more principled than they actually were, at least they were recognizing the desirability of being honest, principled, and so on. The standards set by the Protestant Ethic at least were *there*.

No code of ethics, though, so far as I know, has included the injunction, "Thou shalt not love money nor revere those who have an abundance thereof." There are very few people who do not give special deference and consideration to the possessors of money in large amounts, and very few very rich people, I imagine, who do not feel that their money is an integral part of them, like their charm or a talent for playing the piano.

But the country *is* aroused over the corruption at the White House. There is still something to build upon.

Sunday, May 20

How to write about my fiftieth class reunion? Thirty-three old women, all asserting how young they feel, and six husbands, five of whom were attractive and one a compulsive talker. Two days of too much good food and considerable drink in crowded and noisy rooms, of congratulatory meetings and reunion rhetoric, of reports of financial need and large gifts, mitigated by the beauty of the campus, the hospitality and enthusiasm of the young president and his charming wife—and, of course, the presence of old friends who are still friends in spite of the strange disguise we all wear.

There were several canes and post-cataract spectacles, much fuzzy white hair, some deafness, but all of us were mentally vigorous. Kay, who has been our president ever since our senior year, had postponed an operation for a new hip until next Tuesday. She looked as beautiful and distinguished as ever, was graceful and humorous and equal to every demand. Some who were overlooked in college have become personalities through their achievements since graduation. About a fourth of the class has died. Of those present, one was a sculptor, one a photographer, three had Ph.D.s; there were three writers, a doctor, a teacher, a couple of librarians, and a number of what we used to call society women, interested in children, grandchildren, and many kinds of volunteer work. All the professionals were retired except the writers and one of the archaeologists. There was a mellow acceptance of one another.

Between meetings we walked about the campus, looked in on the new library, chatted in our headquarters, took naps. The things we talked about were, on the whole, rather superficial. At our class dinner we had some present-day students who played and sang some of the new college songs and answered questions about the life of the college today.

There is a popular cliché to the effect that as we get older we must keep our minds "open to new ideas." Ideas new to us, I take this to mean, for absolutely new ideas are rare and hard to come by. I went with my mind wide open, with all my tentacles out for new ideas. I did not find many, for the theme of the whole weekend was money, which the college, like other "independent colleges," needs desperately—and that is a tired old idea if ever there was one.

We learned from our undergraduates that except for the academic rules about cheating in one's work there are no rules in the college now. Men come and go at will. Students may have cats but not dogs; perhaps the cats make that rule. In the newer fireproof dormitories students may smoke anywhere. They may have liquor in their rooms. They may play their stereos all night long. If a student finds another's stereo too loud at 3 a.m. she does not invoke an impersonal "quiet hours" rule but goes to the offender and "confronts" her directly. One or the other gives in. All this is a new idea to me and one I do not embrace. I am glad that I don't have to live in a dormitory now. Asthma from cats, not to mention the smells they can create, a man in the bathroom cubicle next to me, loud rock music at 3 a.m., cigarette smoke in the air, liquor to buy out of a small budget if one is to hold one's own with one's friends: it sounds to me like the triumph of the selfish over the unselfish.

We broke up after lunch today. Some are looking forward to future reunions, the fifty-fifth, the sixtieth, even the sixty-fifth. Two members of 1907, indomitable, were there in wheelchairs. I shall not attend any more, nor will Kay, she says, nor Sophie. It was a good reunion, perhaps the best we have had, and for that reason it is well to end on it. Later we shall be putting a brave face on age; now we are enjoying its rewards.

From now on we live *sub specie aeternitatis*. We have made our contribution, whatever it is; we are on the threshold of a great change, whatever it may be. Today we live in today's sunshine, today's rain, today's love, today's service.

Exactly when did I decide to go to Kendal when it opens? The day that I paid my first substantial deposit—which is still revocable—or the day I wrote in my diary, "Kendal looks like a good thing"?

Preparing to move, even with several months to do it in, is a big undertaking. Fran Smith, having just done it, writes me, "Don't ever move. It's hell."

I am glad that I am making my final move comparatively early, for I am sure that with each year it becomes more traumatic. I remember how disturbed, for several months afterward, both Mother and Violet were, Mother at seventy-five, Violet at seventy-seven. And at both those times I was there, comparatively young and strong, to take responsibility and supply most of the energy. I shall make this move at seventy-one, unassisted.

An antique dealer came today and bought the fireplace things and also a little table that Mother picked up in the Blue Ridge before I was born for a dollar and a half. He paid seventy-eight dollars for it. On the other hand, the six dining-room chairs, bench-made in the 1890s of Honduras mahogany, went for much less than they cost originally. I have no room for them if I keep the rush-bottomed Hitchcock chairs with the original paint, which I much prefer. The things the antique people really want, of course, are those I shall take with me to my new apartment.

I learn something from each man who comes. The things that people collect! Of the hundred and fifty dollars' worth of odd bits and pieces of silver and china, the highest value was put on the souvenir spoon with the Union soldier on it that Violet bought as a child when she was taken to Gettysburg. She paid for it herself with her saved-up allowance, and the cost must have been minuscule. She used to laugh at her childish taste and also at the Union soldiers of the same design that stand on the green in many New England villages. They were, she said, the first examples of mass production. But my antique dealer had a customer in mind who collects silver spoons with whole figures on them.

Victorian beer steins are in great demand now, and he was sorry that I had none of them. I can remember seeing them on plate rails in dining rooms when I was a child and thinking how ugly and old-fashioned they were. But my beautiful and commodious mahogany sideboard, which is in perfect condition, is scorned because it is Empire.

Sunday, May 27

I enjoy my Sundays. They begin with a leisurely breakfast with ginger marmalade for my toast, then a half hour of meditation in preparation for Meeting, then Meeting itself. Usually I have lunch or dinner with some friend. Sue Yarnall and I used to go regularly to Valley Green or the Evergreen for Sunday lunch. I miss her.

In the afternoon I have a go at the Sunday *New York Times*, all six pounds of it (weighed on the bathroom scale). The advertisements annoy me, there are so many of

143

them, with only a tiny trickle of print on a page—a pennyworth of bread to a monstrous deal of sack. But the Week in Review, the Book Review, the Editorials and the Op-Ed page, the Magazine, the Entertainment and Travel sections—these I can't afford to miss.

I find as I get older that I am more, not less, interested in what is happening in the world. It is an unspeakable relief no longer to have to read, shuddering, the latest war news. The characteristics of the different countries have a never-ending fascination; to see people behave in character is always intensely interesting. The Jews never seem able to learn from experience—and I am thinking of their experience in Palestine with the Canaanites and the Hittites and that lot. The Arabs are always so terrifyingly fanatic, the English indomitably decent (except, of course, about Ireland), the Irish passionate about their seventeenth-century religious dissensions. And the United States? A schoolroom full of wildly unruly individuals getting away with murder and the faculty throwing up its hands, the captain of the football team insane.

Thursday, May 31

I drove through the country to Kendal to see how the place where I shall spend the rest of my life was shaping. It was a dazzling spring day, everything green and lush and shining after weeks of rain. The over-all color of the countryside now is green and white; honey locusts dripped their white blossoms and their fragrance everywhere, and along the roadsides sprawled the white blossoms of wild black-

144

berries. In old-fashioned gardens snowball bushes and mock orange blossomed. A small white house tucked under a hillside surrounded by a white picket fence with a white car beside it resembled a large white flower.

It was perhaps the worst possible day to look at Kendal, for the hills of mud and the deep-rutted roads had not had time to dry. Huge machines ground noisily back and forth; "Keep Off" and "Keep Out" signs sprouted everywhere, but in front of the sample apartments blades of new grass printed the soil with green, and a steady stream of prospective inhabitants flowed in and out.

This is actually the second lot of samples: what we are really going to get. The first lot represented the ideal. The chief difference, however, is the substitution of plastic for wood in relatively unimportant places. The living room and bedroom are of adequate size, there is generous closet space, and the kitchen is big enough for a window and a table with two chairs beside it—actually the nicest kitchen I have had in twenty years.

I wondered if the quadrangles on which the apartments face are as wide as I had expected. The storage sheds for terrace furniture also serve as barriers between apartments, providing privacy from one's neighbors alongside, but those who live directly across the green are well within sight and sound. Will people be wandering across on impulse to pay a visit when one comes out on one's terrace?

It will be good, of course, to have friends close at hand—Elizabeth and Jeanie, Fran, Emily, and some of the Poets—and friends can be told that one wants to keep one's mornings for work. But will casual acquaintances drop in or telephone in the morning to arrange committee meetings and make dinner appointments, to suggest a walk or to ask for transportation to village or market?

I have had six years of living entirely alone with only my own wishes and moods to consult. Shall I be adaptable enough for such a close community?

After I left Kendal, I tooled up Baltimore Pike to Swarthmore College and spent two or three hours in the Friends Historical Library, which has much good material on Whittier. It is nearer to Kendal than it was to Alden Park—a plus mark for Kendal.

Sunday, June 3

"What we fear most about death, I believe," writes John Yungblut in *Rediscovering Prayer*, "is the possible loss of our identity forever."

I think—though it is easy to deceive oneself—that I do not have this fear. What I fear is not death but illness—the paralysis following stroke, the agony of cancer, the long weariness of waiting and being cared for while deteriorating mentally and physically. As to the loss of identity, I have had two experiences that take away that fear.

One occurred in late 1938 or early 1939. I had been at Pendle Hill Summer School, where Gerald Heard talked about meditation. I had read and studied *The Cloud of Unknowing* (what an exciting and mind-expanding book that was!), Evelyn Underhill's great book on mysticism, and some books on Eastern religion. I was getting up early

146

in the mornings and practicing meditation not very satisfactorily, mostly losing the battle with distractions. One morning, however, for I do not know how long, I was suddenly outside time and outside myself. I *knew*, in an entirely different way from any other knowing, what it means when we say that God is love. I was beyond my own identity, and yet I was intensely conscious. I felt no regret for the loss of personality; my awareness was of meaning, of love.

The other experience was a series of dreams six or seven years ago. Perhaps five times over a period of a year I dreamed that I was dying. I would wake up with my heart beating wildly, convinced that these were my last moments, and I would consciously prepare myself for death. After a while—how long?—I would realize that this was only a dream, and I would go to sleep again. The final time, however, was an experience of pure happiness. I arranged my nightgown and pillows in a seemly fashion, folded my hands upon my breast, and waited in a sort of cradle of bliss. Nothing happened. After a while I turned on my side, disappointed. I have not had the dream since.

What is the meaning of these dreams? An unacknowledged death wish? Or something physical, such as an attack of palpitations of the heart, which my mind rationalized in this way? Or was it an intuition of truth?

Friday, June 8. Hot and humid

For several years now it has seemed that technology with its machines and computers was taking over our life and

147

men were becoming dwarfed and even obsolescent, but recently in the Skylab Project man has suddenly triumphed. For all the elaborate, infinitely programmed, computerized, mechanized aspects of it, it would have come to nothing if it had not been for the courage, knowledge, and ability to improvise of the individual men engaged in it.

When the great tube overheated, the men inside communicated with men on the ground 270 miles below. They rigged up a nylon sunshade and with great daring fastened it in place. After they had been living inside this incredibly cramped laboratory for two weeks, the batteries began to run down. One of the astronauts climbed outside the Skylab and, clinging to its surface, pried loose the wings that had stuck and got the batteries to charging again.

One man's hands and muscles are as necessary to voyages of discovery in the space age as they were when a sailor climbed the rigging of the *Santa María* in 1492.

Tuesday, June 12

The tenth day of our current Bermuda high. We usually have one in June—day after day of sunny, hot, humid weather—and each year I think that this particular one is the longest and the hottest ever. As I drove home through Penn Valley, it seemed to me that the trees, the shady lawns with their splotches of sunshine like gold coins, the expensive shrubbery, all looked as if they had been coated

148

with yellow Vaseline, oily and shiny. I have noticed this look in other summers; it comes with this particular kind of intense and prolonged heat. It makes me long for New England and the dry airy spaces under the high limbs of the elms. I hope it is cooler tomorrow, for Fran comes off the *France* from chilly England in her tweed suit. She leaves in January, taking with her clothes for winter and spring in a climate where a temperature of 78 constitutes a "sweltering heat wave."

I am still working on Sunday's *N.Y.T.* In a very interesting interview Dame Helen Gardner talks about literature in connection with growing old. From the age of forty, she says, one ceases to be responsive to new aesthetic experiences. Forty seems to me to be young for the cut-off date. I'm not sure that this is true for me at the age of seventy. I responded wholly to *Godspell*, for instance. She says she reads modern poetry, but it does not stay in her mind. I wonder if it stays in the minds of young people either. It has no rhyme or meter to hook into the memory, and the poems are often so private that there are no firm ideas to grasp. There is only an emotion evoked by the poem, and that passes.

Of the consolations of age, she says:

> You gain knowledge of yourself and the world. In some ways anxiety and ambition are painful and they die. . . . When I was young you were made to do things you did not want to do. I hated going to dances. I just *loathed* dancing. I was hopeless at tennis. In that period I used to say to myself a passsge from

Agamemnon. Clytemnestra says to the assembled elders of Argos: "In time men grow dead to feelings of shame." I thought, the time will come when I shan't mind that I don't play tennis. I shall just do what I want to and enjoy doing it.

Unfortunately shame does not disappear. It simply finds different things to feed on. Forgetfulness, for instance. I am stricken with shame when I inconvenience other people—and make myself ridiculous—by forgetting appointments. Is there something one can do, I wonder, about one's memory? Some exercise to strengthen it? Is it a good thing to make lists and write notes to oneself, or does this increase the flabbiness of mental muscles? Or is it simply that brain cells die and are not replaced?

"Shieling." Wednesday, June 20

Settling in for the summer in the dear Studio made from the old carriage house at the end of Elizabeth's barn.

Violet and I came first to Shieling to have lunch with Elizabeth and Bill McGreal in 1954 on our way home from Mount Desert. That was only three years after Elizabeth's winning of the Newbery Award for *Amos Fortune, Free Man* and six years before *The Lighted Heart*, in which she wrote of Bill, their buying of the two-hundred-year-old farmhouse on the edge of Peterborough, and their courageous adjustment to life as it was restricted by Bill's encroaching blindness.

The place is full of Bill, though he died almost ten years

150

ago. He did his work for the New Hampshire Association for the Blind in the little office, made from an old icehouse, where I now work in the mornings. With his Shetland sheep dog, Tawn, at his side, he walked freely over lawn and garden. In the house, or on the porch looking toward Pack Monadnock, he was always the center of the group, keenly interested in whatever was afoot. And always Elizabeth, strong and beautiful, was there, ready to say the word that would forestall a collision or a misunderstanding but never proffering unneeded help.

On the other side of the farmhouse is Pine-Apple Cottage, where Elizabeth's sprightly English friend, Nora Unwin, illustrates Elizabeth's books and her own, paints, and teaches painting at the Sharon Art Center. The famous MacDowell Colony is on the other side of Peterborough; we have our own colony here.

Tuesday, June 26

Three afternoons a week I go over to Elizabeth's house and watch the Senate Watergate hearings. They've been going on for weeks and will last, it seems, weeks longer. There is a horrible fascination about them. And occasionally something good comes through. Today a young man admitted that he had lied, saying that he did it out of fear of the group and long-standing loyalty to the President. Senator Baker interrupted him. "I think the greatest disservice a man can do to the Presidency is to abdicate his conscience."

It was good to hear conscience mentioned.

151

A pair of rose-breasted grosbeaks must be nesting nearby. They come regularly to my feeder. I have seen the brilliant male bird only two or three times in my life before; now I see him several times a day. The female, too, is interesting, with her clear brown and white markings.

Wednesday, June 27

I spoke to the Whittier Society of Haverhill this afternoon at its seventy-seventh summer meeting in The Birthplace. (They refer to The Birthplace as if it were The Manger.) Rain poured down in torrents, but still between fifty and sixty people turned out to sit on folding wooden chairs in the barn. It is a functioning barn, with hay in the loft and the caretaker's bull on a lower level, so that there was a rich warm barn odor, pastoral and nostalgic. I liked it. What I did not like was the sharply contrasting, blinding light directly in my eyes for the videotape recording. In this electronic age no one asks me if I am willing to have this sort of record made of my talk to be used on the local TV station.

Perhaps four or five men were in the audience, the three younger ones all bearded. All three came up and spoke to me afterward. My title was "Whittier and Rufus Jones," and all these men had known R. M. J. at Haverford or Oak Grove School or the American Friends Service Committee. There was also a small boy, the grandson of the president of the Society, a beautiful lad of ten or thereabouts, who looked rather like a Hugh Thompson illustration, with thick, taffy-colored bangs down to his eye-

152

brows. He had long, thoughtful gray eyes and a wide mouth, with an expression of tenderness unusual in a small boy. He listened seriously to the talk and when he was introduced to me afterward gave me a fleeting smile.

(There is something mannered and old-fashioned about the word "lad," and yet it sounds right for this particular boy. I must look it up in the dictionary to see if it is marked "obs." I must buy a new dictionary, for I did not bring one, thinking I had left my old Desk Thorndike behind last summer. I could live for three months without a Bible but not without a dictionary.)

All the time I was talking, the rain poured down outside the open door and drummed on the roof. Afterward we ran from the barn to the house, leaping puddles as we went, to eat strawberry shortcake draped with mantles of real whipped cream, under the piercing sidewise gaze of the poet Whittier on the wall.

Friday, June 29

The "hate list" of the White House has come out in the Watergate hearings, a long list of distinguished people: ambassadors, including John Kenneth Galbraith, senators, newspaper people, writers, and entertainment figures, who are to be given trouble in various ways. A notation beside one name, for instance, was: "A scandal would help here." Most of them, though, were to have their income taxes audited by the IRS.

The whole thing is disturbing, but one aspect not mentioned by anyone is perhaps the most disturbing of all: the

153

assumption underlying it all that *everyone* cheats on his in-
come-tax returns and that all these people are therefore
going to be seriously embarrassed by such an audit. I do
not cheat on my income tax, and I believe that most people don't.

Saturday, June 30

I have just bought a dictionary, Webster's New Collegiate
Dictionary, copyright 1973. It includes a handbook of
style with forms of address. How to write to the Pope, for
instance, to a foreign ambassador, to an American ambassador (one is an excellency, the other an honorable), to a
chief justice and a general. But not to a Crown Prince. People will have to come to me for that. I got a letter from
my Crown Prince yesterday and answered it at once.

The word "lad" is not obsolete. To my surprise, it is
designated, in its second meaning, "informal."

One can spend a lot of time poring over a new dictionary. I looked up all the four-letter words I could think
of, and they are all there. After people have used these
words, as they are doing now, until all the nap has worn
off them and they are threadbare of meaning, what will be
left to use when there is really a need to shock people into
attention?

There are fairly numerous line drawings. I think the
roadrunner looks more like a mockingbird, but perhaps
this is caviling. There is a picture of a settle and one of a
settee.

Many abbreviations are included—that is, series of let-

154

ters: for instance, NAACP, BBC, KP, SST. There are some words from foreign languages, including Japanese words and Indian. An *obi* is there and also a *sari*. On the other hand, a *yogi* is there but not a *roshi*. Words that should begin with capital letters do, and the others are in lower case. Some dictionaries put all words in caps, which is exasperating.

While there are many proper names in the main text, such as Joseph of Arimathea, Robin Hood, Rob Roy (a Manhattan made with Scotch whisky, not the Scottish outlaw), there are also separate lists for Biographical Names and Geographical Names. It does not distinguish between whiskey and whisky, though George Stevens thought me very ignorant because I did not know which was Scotch and which bourbon. And now I have forgotten what he told me. But it describes a whiskey sour in detail. It seems to me adequate on drinks. I have looked up stinger, Bloody Mary, screwdriver, and gimlet. It does not have Pym or Pym no. 1, which I enjoyed in England with borage in it.

It has Bo Tree but says nothing about its connection with the Buddha. Togo and Tojo are in the Biographical list, but not Dr. Taisetz Suzuki, a far greater man than either; Yamamoto and Yamashita are there, but not Michi Kawai, Noboko Hani, Ume Tsuda, or Etsu Sugimoto. Lady Murasaki got in, but I can't find any other Japanese women. Hiroshige, the artist, is there, but not Basho, the poet. The list is strongest on statesmen, generals, and admirals.

155

Shortly after I had looked up Yamamoto Isoroku (the man who planned the attack on Pearl Harbor, though the dictionary identified him only as "Jap. admiral"), the mail came with a letter from his son, Tadao! He wrote that he had been playing tennis with the Crown Prince. They must have spoken of me, for I have letters from both of them written on the same day, though Tadao's came a day later. They planned, he said, to play tennis every morning, but as it was the rainy season, they could play only two days. "But it is rather comfortable for me, because we are old enough [he means too old] to run hard!" These young men—whom I still think of as schoolboys—are pushing forty now!

Wednesday, July 4

Showers all day. Elizabeth and I went to the Acre, her lovely wooded retreat on Hunts Pond, between downpours, and it had its own beauty, the trees so green, the mist rising from the still pond, the silence, except for wood thrushes and now and then a blue jay.

Peterborough's Fourth of July celebration, usually so spirited and traditional, was missing this year. The old cannon blew up last year, and someone has stolen the flag. The Declaration of Independence, which is usually read, is intact, but they passed it by. Why, I wonder.

Saturday, July 7

After the fortnight of rain, with occasional hot, steamy interludes, suddenly the air is clear and dry, stimulating as wine. Last night for the first time since I have been here I saw the stars, the Big Dipper swinging low, Arcturus overhead, Jupiter like a lamp in the southeastern sky.

This morning I walked across the field on the narrow path through the tall grass, the purple alfalfa blossoms, and the yellow hop clover. Wide swathes of grass had been flattened by the heavy rain in irrational curves at the whim of the wind. I went through the pines and down the hill to the clamorous brook, up through the woods on the other side to the small old sugar house under the big maples. The woods were wet and mosquitoes buzzed, but ovenbirds were calling, "Teacher! Teacher!" and a wood thrush was singing. On the way back I detoured to the fence to look at the meadow where horses were grazing, at the rolling slopes of green with a rock here and there, the clump of elms, the puffy clouds in the blue sky. It was full summer, rich, satisfying. Whittier could describe such a New England scene perfectly.

Saturday, July 14

In George Santayana's *America*, a book of essays first published in periodicals, there is one called "Shakespeare Made in America," in which the sonnet "When, in disgrace with fortune and men's eyes" is rewritten in modern images, with all the references to courts and kings deleted and appropriate Americanisms substituted. "And trouble deaf heaven with my bootless cries" becomes, "Doubting if

God can hear me when I pray." It says again what has been on my mind lately: that our religious symbols are worn out.

Today we feel no awe before kings or the thought of them. We kindly say that they—or such remnants of them as are left—are as human as we are. Majesty has no emotional impact on us. Shepherds are quaintly obsolete. Even what kings and shepherds stand for, authority and protection, awaken no feelings of respect or gratitude. Authority rests in the people, security in an elected and imperfect government. The stars in the entertainment world seem to arouse the most general excited interest, and probably most people secretly, if not openly, give respect to those who have a great deal of money. But this is hardly religious awe. Perhaps the symbol from the lovely twelfth-century English carol, "Jesus our brother, kind and good," is the one that stands up best.

But it may be that the capacity really to worship is a rare one in any age.

Sunday, July 15

To the Lyceum at the Unitarian Church. James McGregor Burns said that if the President cannot come forward with a convincing statement that clears it all up, he should be impeached. He talked about impeachment as a surgical operation, about the possibility of Nixon's being cleared, the stagnation of the government at present, and so on. Having made these statements very strongly and clearly, he went on to other things. In the question period afterward a man got up and asked, "What do you think of the idea of impeaching the President?" People simply do not listen.

The Lyceum talks are so good. There are eight during the summer, given by seven men and one woman. I am to be the token woman on August 12. I am getting scared. *Why* did I ever say I'd do it?

Wednesday, July 18

Oliver Wendell Holmes, Jr., on words: "A word is not a crystal, transparent and unchanged; it is the skin of a living thought and may vary greatly in color and content according to the circumstances and the time in which it is used." This is an interesting idea about words and quite opposed to the anonymous verse that I have treasured these many years:

> *The written word should be*
> *Clean as a bone,*
> *Clear as a crystal,*
> *Hard as a stone.*
> *Two words are not*
> *So good as one.*

On his ninetieth birthday Holmes made a little talk about running races and continuing his work and then quoted a fourth-century Latin poet (who?): "Death plucks my ear and says, Live—I am coming "

This is great. He had four more years to live, and he lived them. There was no collapse after his retirement. To live right up to the end and still to welcome the end: this is what I should like to do.

Holmes again: "If I were dying, my last words would be, Have faith and pursue the unknown end."

Friday, July 20

This afternoon at the Acre I took the kayak out. It isn't the real thing, being from Sears and plastic and almost as wide as the canoe, but still it is tippy.

The pond was absolutely smooth at sunset. There were no speedboats, and only a beaver on the far side giving an occasional mighty splash. The kayak moved lightly, softly, with almost no effort of the long, double-blade paddle. I felt a solemn joy as I moved over the water, the bow nosing slightly to one side and then the other, and I felt as I had as a child when I first paddled a canoe alone.

It was at Elmira, New York, on the Chemung River. Mother—who also went with me when I first took out my Model T Ford on my own—was my passenger. As we slowly moved upstream, she quoted from her favorite "Launcelot and Elaine":

> ". . . *the dead,*
> *Oar'd by the dumb, went upward with the flood.*"

Saturday, July 21

Older people like to have their picnics on chairs at tables, and I know why. At the Acre on Thursday evening we sat on the ground at the edge of the pond. The scene was

160

lovely, the breath of air off the water refreshing, the talk lively. I sat at a strained angle on a sloping rock, and after a while I became conscious of an intermittent pain under my left shoulder. I got up and moved about, but as the evening wore on, the pain increased in intensity. That night I was having muscle spasms every thirty seconds. The aspirin I took had no effect.

So as I tossed in bed I thought about pain. John Yungblut in *Rediscovering Prayer* says it is possible to relax into pain, to *be* the pain. This sounds reasonable, especially in cases of muscle spasm, for any attempt to fight it simply stiffens the muscles and intensifies the pain. I tried it and perhaps it helped. Eventually I slept.

Some people have a low threshold of pain, it is said, others a high. Some are far more stoic about enduring it. Do they feel it less? How do you measure degrees of pain? Is the person who whimpers or cries out feeling more pain than the silent, tight-lipped one? Does the mental attitude of the stoic reduce the pain?

The Japanese make a great point of enduring pain bravely, and they make very little use of anesthetics. When my young friend Pierre went through the windshield of a taxi in Tokyo and a Japanese doctor sewed up his lacerated face so skillfully that no scar resulted, Pierre was given no anesthetic at all, and the pain was excruciating. When Princess Kazuko, years ago, had a tooth topped and the casing was driven in around the root, she had no anesthetic and made no sound, only gripped Miss Natori's hand very tight. Everyone admired her courage—

and no one thought she might just as well have had Novo-
cain and been spared that ordeal. Childbirth in Japan is
"natural" without benefit of exercises and preparation beforehand. It is taken for granted that people will endure
pain bravely.

Pride no doubt helps. But whatever the expression of it,
or the suppression of expression, the pain itself remains
and the endurance of it is the problem of each individual.
The old person must expect pain. Arthritis, angina, broken bones, cancer are common in the later years. There are
drugs which legitimately help, but there are limits to their
efficacy. At seventy I try to look this knowledge in the
face.

But now, more than ever before, one begins to live one
moment at a time. Perhaps in all things, joy as well as
pain, this is the attitude the old must cultivate.

Monday, July 23

Some moderns are indignant because Whittier was not an
admirer of Walt Whitman. They died in the same year,
1892, but Walt was twelve years younger than Whittier—
and Walt was a modern. Walt admired Whittier and
would have liked to be friends, but he said he had it "on
good authority" that Whittier threw *Leaves of Grass* into
the fire. There is absolutely no proof of that. Walt did not
name his "authority," and the only possible evidence is
that there was no copy of the book in Whittier's library.

There *is* evidence that Whittier tried to like Whitman.
Whenever he referred to him he spoke approvingly of his

162

work in the hospitals in Washington during the Civil War, and he praised the younger man's poems on Lincoln. Though Whittier himself had no horse, he contributed ten dollars to a subscription for a horse and buggy for Whitman, to whom he referred as "the old fellow." He advocated getting a sober, trustworthy horse, which was done. Whitman promptly exchanged him for a fast stepper—and was run away with.

I opened my copy of *Leaves of Grass* to read it, if I could, with Whittier's eyes. Almost the first thing I came on was: "I dote on myself, there is that lot of me and all so luscious." How could Whittier like that—Whittier who sought and to a great degree achieved selflessness?

Tuesday, July 24

I read the notes that come from the Shakespeare Theatre at Stratford, Connecticut, before driving down there to see the plays. In those on *The Country Wife* (Wycherley) I find: "By the end of the play [Margery] joins them because she can't beat them . . . so that to a certain extent it's a very moral play because it shows a picture of society where innocence cannot win—it just *cannot* win."

Now why is that a moral play? Is the defeat of simple goodness moral? I have recourse to the dictionary.

INNOCENCE: 1,a: freedom from guilt or sin through being unacquainted with evil: BLAMELESSNESS b: chastity c: freedom from legal guilt of a particular crime or offense d(1): freedom from guile or cunning: SIMPLICITY (2): lack of worldly experience or sophistication e: lack of knowledge.

Perhaps it is the lack of knowledge that is operative here. A person might not have been virtuous had he been exposed to temptation or to the attractions and pitfalls of evil. In Buddhism the crucial sin is ignorance, the ultimate highest experience is enlightenment. One has the duty to know. Is that why it is moral to show that innocence cannot win?

Thursday, July 26

Back from my annual binge at Stratford. Is it the tenth time? Elizabeth and Jeanie as usual drove up from Swarthmore and met me there. The plays were *Macbeth*, *Measure for Measure*, and *The Country Wife*. All of them were played so as to bring out the evil in man. Power-crazed man met downfall and death in *Macbeth* with agonized comments on "our poor country" by other characters. In *Measure for Measure* a narrow moralist tried to cure a corrupt society by harsh measures and failed through his own vulnerability to temptation. *The Country Wife* depicted a licentious and sex-crazed superficial society to which the innocent country girl capitulated with pleasure. There is one enchanting scene having to do with a letter.

I like *Measure for Measure* least of Shakespeare's plays. I saw it in Stratford, England, in 1962, well done in the traditional way. It was interesting to see it again in this year of Watergate, with all of the implications for modern society stressed by the staging, but it is still a repellent play. I can't remember how many times I have seen *Macbeth*. It moves me deeply every time. There were no kilts

164

in this production; all the costumes were stark black or dazzling white or blood red. The witches were three court ladies—a fascinating touch.

Monday, July 30

Again to the Whittier Collection in Haverhill's fine new library, where I spent so much time last summer, to check once more on Whittier's love affair with Elizabeth Lloyd. There are two books, Marie Denervaud's *Whittier's Unknown Romance* and Thomas Franklin Currier's *Elizabeth Lloyd and the Whittiers*, in which the letters between the two are collected. In Martha Hale Shackford's *Whittier and the Cartlands*, published after the first two books, Whittier is quoted as saying that Elizabeth Lloyd was the only woman he ever really loved but that he could not marry her because of his ill health and because he had his mother and sister to support. Biographers have either accepted that at face value or they have found obscure—and I think improbable—psychological explanations for his bachelorhood. I have my own theory.

They were friends from the time Whittier was thirty and Elizabeth twenty-six. He was in no position to marry when he was young, with his mother and sister to support and no job that paid more than nine hundred dollars a year. Moreover, Elizabeth was the exquisitely pretty daughter of rich and conservative Philadelphia Quakers who did not approve of abolitionism or of Whittier's liberal Quakerism. But the two were undoubtedly drawn to each other, and they exchanged letters from time to time

165

for years. A day or two before her marriage at forty-two she wrote a revealing little note to him saying that she would be in all day and would see him at any time.

After her husband's death three years later, they met again in Philadelphia and for three weeks evidently saw each other every day. Then she went to Elmira to take the fashionable water cure, and letters flew back and forth at the rate of three a week. In one of them he wrote:

> Elizabeth, I have been happy—far more than I ever expected in this life. The sweet memory of the past few weeks makes me rich forever. What Providence has in store for the future I know not—I dare not hope scarcely—but the past is mine—may I not say ours—sacred and beautiful, a joy forever. Asking nothing of thee,—and with the tenderest regard for thy griefs and memories, I have given thee what was thine by right—the love of an honest heart—not as a restraint and burden upon thee,—imposing no obligation and calling for no solicitude on thy part as respects myself. Nobody is a loser by loving or being loved.

But then he went back to Amesbury, where he and his sister Lizzie had been living, and a little less than three months later Elizabeth Lloyd was writing to him accusing him of having changed. He wrote back: "If there has been any change in the letters, I am sure there is no change in the feeling which dictated them, so far as *thou* art concerned." Then he spoke of old feelings of self-distrust, of inability to make those he loved happy, of his age, his "old-fashioned and homely" daily habits, his limitations. "I am sure thy fine artist-nature would pine and die under the hard and uncongenial influences which make me what I am, and from which I cannot escape without feeling that I have abandoned the post of duty, without losing my self-respect, and forfeiting all right to be loved in return by those I love."

He had not yet written *Snow-Bound*, which was the beginning of his financial success, but he was publishing poems regularly in the *Atlantic Monthly* and being paid for them. His mother and his aunt had died; he and his sister were living quite comfortably in Amesbury, and Elizabeth Lloyd had inherited money from her father and her husband. Why did they not marry now? She obviously would have welcomed it.

Undoubtedly he felt out of her world, but he was not the obscure homespun Quaker he might seem to himself to be. He was among the great, with whom he was entirely at ease. I think there was another reason. I think Lizzie could not bear the idea. They had been so close, such dear friends as well as brother and sister; she was not well and she was dependent upon him financially as well as emotionally. "Dear Lizzie is ill," he wrote to Elizabeth Lloyd, and dear Lizzie was in a "deep depression." Months later, after the matter had been resolved and Elizabeth Lloyd had asked him to burn her letters, he wrote her: "Dear Lizzie is feeling better."

Iris Murdoch is one of the few women novelists whom the critics take seriously. In *The Black Prince* she says, speaking in her own person as author, not as one of her characters: "Life is horrible, without metaphysical sense, wrecked by chance, pain and the close prospect of death."

She states this opinion with more pungency than most people, perhaps, but she is not alone in her view. Indeed it seems to me that it has become a modern cliché, with no more truth than most clichés. Unquestionably there is much pain, physical and mental, in the world. We can never forget the anguish of those who suffered in the German death camps, at Hiroshima and Nagasaki, in the villages of Vietnam: the three great crimes of the modern world. And pain goes on in prisons, ghettos, labor camps, in bombed villages and places where political prisoners are tortured. But pain is not cumulative. It is individual. When an individual has too much to bear, he is eased by death, which comes as a friend. And no one's life is wholly pain; each has some moments of beauty, of happiness.

To me it seems childish and churlish to say that life is horrible and without meaning. Life is a trust, given into our hands, to hold carefully, to use well, to enjoy, to give back when the time comes. Oh, I know I have been fortunate beyond most people and far beyond my deserts. Perhaps I lack that "tragic sense" which Europeans are said to have and in which Americans are reported to be deficient. I do not think that life lacks metaphysical sense, even if I cannot say explicitly what that sense is, and I am sure that life has meaning, that I have work to do, that when it is finished I shall abandon this body and enter the unknown.

Meanwhile there is the beauty of the sunrise, of a misty, salty sea coast with the bell buoy intoning, of a great pine tree against the sky. There is the deep joy of friendship, of human love, the challenge of writing, the excitement of watching the world careening on its way, the small steady comforts of cold water, of bed, of a shower bath, of a new-laid egg, and hot coffee; the stimulus of books and reading and ideas that stir one to agreement or rejection or question.

Saturday, August 4

Donald Hall, a young poet, writes in his introduction to the Laurel Edition of Whittier's poems:

> Robinson was convinced that life was pretty much a bad thing. To me as to most moderns Robinson's view is more convincing than Whittier's, but this is to be expected, for Robinson's negativism is the weather of our times. To read Whittier requires an effort of the historical imagination; we must learn to cope with goodness and optimism.

Two in two days!

Tuesday, August 7

I went into the attractive new bookstore in town, run by a very young man with a band around his head, a mop of bushy, tangled hair, and a ragged brown mustache. I bought a book for a friend's birthday, and then, noticing a shelf with a large sign, "Books by Local Authors," I said, "You could have some of my books on that shelf, for I spend my summers here."

He said, "What is your name?"

I told him, mentioning titles of books, and he answered, "I've never heard of you."

This was a shock. Here was, I realized quickly, another example of the advent of age. In any bookshop run by a middle-aged woman I should have been known, but this was a. young man, too young to have read the newspaper accounts of my going to Japan, not interested in my kind of novel.

On the table at which he sat there was a copy of one of Taisetz Suzuki's books on Zen. I lingered a moment or two, talking about Dr. Suzuki, for I did not want to leave the store abruptly, as if angered by not being recognized. Also I thought that the fact I had known Dr. Suzuki well and could talk about him as a person might interest a man who was trying to sell Suzuki's books.

It did not. He stared at me and made no comment. I said good-by and left.

It was a disturbing experience. Even an embarrassed young man should be able to rally and make some effort to retrieve the situation, to look interested and responsive even if he did not feel so. Any up-and-coming bookstore, moreover, should be aware of speakers coming to the local Lyceum and be prepared to seize the occasion to sell their

170

books. This wholly lethargic young man seemed to me to be courting failure—and I hate to see bookstores fail.

On the personal level, there was the obvious fact that I was, after a lifetime of writing and a few outstanding successes, totally unknown to a person whose business it was to know books. Something like this happens, I have no doubt, to retired heads of organizations who go back expecting to be received with the respect and excitement that they once took for granted and find that the bright young executives do not know their names. It is a kind of death, a foretaste of the total disregard and anonymity that will cover us as the tide covers and obliterates a sand castle.

Wednesday, August 8. Sunny, hot, and humid

I drove to Amesbury, Massachusetts, to see Mr. Roland Woodwell, who lives on Whitehall Road, up the hill from the Whittier homestead on Friend Street. Mr. Woodwell has lived all his life in Amesbury, where he taught in the high school, and for forty years of it he has been collecting material on Whittier for his definitive biography, now finished. He is trying to find a publisher for his 1600 typed pages. Everybody who writes about Whittier goes to see him.

He lives in a pleasant frame house filled with antiques but not cluttered, high on a hill overlooking the river, Whittier's "broad and lovely Merrimac," and the bay. On clear days he can see Cape Ann, but today the heat haze hid the distances. He is a spare, spidery old gentleman (how old? My age. Ha!), rather courtly in a spare New

England way. He lives alone in his wax-neat house. Seven years ago his aunt, who used to live with him, died.

He apologized for his study, which is upstairs overlooking the view. It is filled to the ceiling with books, but I thought it neat and clean. He said that he used to beg his aunt to keep out of it and not to clean it. Once he gave her ten dollars for a favorite charity on the condition that she stay out of his study for a month. She reported this at a meeting of the board of the charity, and they all clapped.

We had a lovely gossip about Whittier. He told me that brother Matthew Franklin's divorce was not recorded and perhaps there had never been one. Nevertheless, he lived for some years in Boston with his "affinity." This must have created quite a stir in those tight-laced times. Whittier in all his letters that I have seen made no reference to it, though he spoke of brother Frank with affection and with sympathy for his hard life. But this is probably one reason why Frank's daughters, Lizzie and Alice, were so often with Whittier in Amesbury.

Mr. Woodwell told me, too, when we were talking about Whittier and Whitman, that a librarian in Amesbury some years ago, hearing that Whittier had thrown *Leaves of Grass* into the fire, said, "To hell with Whittier," and refused for the rest of the time he was in Amesbury to buy anything at all about Whittier for the library. Since then they have had to fill in the gaps in their Whittier collection at considerable expense.

I said I did not believe that Whittier had thrown *L of G* into the fire; there was no evidence, and it was unlike him.

172

"No," said Mr. Woodwell, "and he had too much respect for his fire to throw a bad book into it. He was very fussy about his fire. No one was allowed to touch it but himself."

Friday, August 10

Hot, hot, hot. The mountain has vanished. Trees and grass are a grayish color. The sky is white. Heat lies damp and heavy on everything, and at night the moon is a burning copper.

Elizabeth and I went blueberry picking on Pitcher Mountain. The whole hill is covered with high bushes blue with berries. Cars park at intervals beside the narrow dirt track and people disappear among the bushes with pails in their hands. The little berries are in clusters of as many as ten. The berries are at first white, then rose, then a deep blue with a gloss on it. At the end of each is a tiny, five-pointed crown.

It was hot, but there was a breeze. There is something about the generosity of the blueberry bush that is moving in a deep and primitive way.

Sunday, August 12

Morning. Before my talk on Whittier at the Summer Lyceum of the Unitarian Church.

Laurie Armstrong just called up to say good morning and to tell me that all the intellectuals in town are boning up on Whittier. I told her that I expected them to stay away in droves. She said May Sarton had telephoned her last night and had sent me her love and best wishes for this morning.

I expect a sparse audience made up of elderly women and my loyal friends. Clara and Phyllis have come from Manchester, Vermont, having spent the night at a motel in order to be here in plenty of time. The Opplers will come over from Marlborough, New Hampshire.

I don't know when I have felt so *cherished* before a speech, certainly not since the New York *Herald Tribune* Forum in 1947. Elizabeth said encouraging words to me in the early morning; Bob Greenleaf will come for me; Nora is going to leave her own church for the only time this summer; there was a dinner party last night, and there will be a luncheon after the speech today.

Later. As it turned out, the church was full—442 people. (Somebody clicked something at the door.) They were attentive, they got every point, laughed when it was appropriate. They were mostly women, of course, but some men came. A Congregational minister from Concord, Massachusetts, with a Sunday off saw the announcement in the *Globe* and brought his wife and daughter.

The party afterward—the main dish at Elizabeth's and the dessert at Laurie's—was great fun. Then I came home and went to bed with *The New York Times*.

Friday, August 17

Last week I told Elizabeth and Laurie about my encounter with the new bookstore. Yesterday Laurie went in there fired with loyalty to do something about it. She asked young Fuzzy Hair for one of my books. He said he would look it up and took down a tome. She went cruising about the shop and came back to say, "You really should have her on the Local Author shelf. She's our most distinguished author."

"Yes," he said, "she came in and told me so."

> *Sit still, my heart, do not raise your dust.*
> *Let the world find its way to you.*
> —Tagore. *Stray Birds*

Saturday, August 18

I like doing the typing of my book myself, because I can make little final changes as I go along. Sometimes I have interesting exchanges with my subconscious mind—with M'Connachie, as Barrie called his, or George, as I. A. R. Wylie named hers.

The other day I made so many bad mistakes in the typing of one page—leaving out a line, not spacing a new paragraph—that I had to redo the page three times. Then I realized that my subconscious was trying to tell me that there was something wrong with the writing itself, not the typing alone. I reread the page carefully, and I saw that I had taken for granted a reader's understanding of material that should be commented on and explained. I wrote a new paragraph to put into the middle of the page, and after that the typing proceeded with only the normal number of correctable errors.

Monday, August 20

Drove to Germantown, 375 miles. The New Jersey Turn-pike on a Monday afternoon is actually frightening. All three lanes are full, and half the vehicles on the road are trucks. The biggest ones roar down the middle lane at seventy miles an hour. If you are so unfortunate as to be in front of one, proceeding at the legal sixty, he comes up close behind you and blinks his lights at you until you find a slot on one side or the other to escape into. The swish and roar of traffic is all but deafening. Evidently traffic accumulates over the weekend, and all of it pours down the road on Monday. This is a day I shall avoid in future.

I have come back to my apartment, which is hot and airless, having been closed for two months, to make the last arrangements for entering Kendal. Just when I made the final decision I am not quite sure, but here I am. Up to now I have known that I could withdraw at will and so was not committed. Now I shall be; to be exact, the day after tomorrow I shall be.

Tuesday, August 21

Spent the day transferring money from savings accounts to checking account. Engaged a moving company to move my things on October thirtieth and reserved a freight elevator in the Manor for that day. This looks final.

Wednesday, August 22

I have spent the night with Elizabeth and Jeanie, who are

having trouble selling their house. Their date for moving into Kendal is October third. This is really worrying for them. A young couple wants the house but cannot get a mortgage.

I went to Kendal and gave them a check, to be held until the checks from the savings banks have had time to be cleared. I could not see the apartment that is to be mine, for all the lower part down near the woods is still a scene of frenetic activity—trucks, digging machines, cranes, piles of dirt. How can they possibly finish it by October first?

A momentous step has been taken, and I poke myself gently to see how I feel, as one touches with a tentative tongue a tooth that might be going to give trouble. When I move on October thirtieth I shall have been at Alden Park six years all but one month. Six to eight years has been the average length of occupation of houses or apartments over my lifetime. That is a lot of moving. One would think I might have acquired a technique, so that I could do it easily and efficiently, but I have only acquired a deeper dread of the process. I feel disorganized and helpless, faced with countless petty decisions.

But apart from all the fuss and fume of moving, I find myself deeply satisfied—and grateful—that I am going to Kendal. The beauty of the surrounding countryside, the pleasant apartments and comfortable arrangements, the prospect of being part of a community where I shall find some of my closest friends and hope to make many more, the opportunity of helping to make it a caring community, and the security for the future: all these are important to me.

As to everybody's being old there, they will, most of them, be young old, enjoying the first exhilaration of retirement. There is a difference between young old and old old. But that stage, too, will come, of course.

Thursday, August 23

Coming back along the New Jersey Turnpike this beautiful Thursday morning, I found only the normal amount of traffic, and that relaxed and good-natured. As I drove along I thought of the time—how many years ago now?—when I met Khrushchev's party on its way to lunch with Johnson in Glassboro.

I had noticed suddenly that there was no traffic at all coming toward me on the other half of the road. It was a strange sight, all three lanes completely empty. Then in the distance I saw six motorcycles across the road ahead with their lights blazing. After them, wheeling along briskly, came a dozen or so large black limousines filled with men in dark suits. It was impossible to tell who was in any one car as they whirled past. Then followed another rank of motorcycles, and after that, at a little distance, the road was solidly full, as far as the eye could reach, with the cars and trucks that had been held up to let the Russian party go through.

The meeting at Glassboro—that little South Jersey town in the pine woods, seat of a small teachers college—was held informally in the unpretentious white frame house of the college president. At the time it was hailed as a breakthrough (the word "détente" not then discovered or invented), a friendly landmark, a typically American affair in its informality and improvisation. As I drove along, remembering it so vividly, I thought of the difference between that and Brezhnev's recent, almost secret visit to Nixon and the way that has been written up as if it were the first and only contact between Soviet Russia and the United States.

Friday, August 24

Beautiful day, cool and sunny. I finished typing my Whittier book this morning, and this afternoon Elizabeth and I went to the Acre, swam and canoed.

Tuesday, August 28

The writer never rests from seeking words to clothe his experience. Last night we had an unusually sharp thunderstorm. I woke up saying to myself, "Delicately articulated thunder, that's it."

The deadline for my book is September first, and this morning I sent the manuscript off. I am not satisfied with the title, "Poet of Freedom," but it will do until I—or my editor—can think of a better one.

When I was young I went through a sort of madness after I had sent off a book—a compound of release, apprehension, elation, despair. I was ready for a trip to a far land, restless, adventurous. Now I am very staid. I look forward without much pleasure to free mornings in which to deal with an accumulation of letters.

Friday, August 31

Dag Hammarskjöld wrote in 1955, *"Respect for the word* is the commandment in the discipline by which a man can be educated to maturity—intellectual, emotional and moral. . . . To misuse the word is to show contempt for man. It undermines the bridges and poisons the wells. It causes Man to regress down the long path of his evolution."

Nearly twenty years later, respect for the word has sunk far lower than he can have imagined.

The Watergate hearings have brought to light an extraordinary tangle of lies and perjuries by people in high office who have sworn to support justice. And not only outright lies but evasions and euphemisms abound throughout government action. "Protective reaction strikes" for aggressive bombing. "Indicate" for say. "Inoperative" for untrue. This is perversion of the language itself. It started perhaps with the exaggerations and distortions of TV advertisements and has crept like a miasma through all our speaking and writing.

Saturday, September 1

We went, Elizabeth and Nora and I, to dinner at Grandmother's House, that incomparable country restaurant overlooking a pond and a family of white geese. Then on to Francestown and the concert in the stately church designed by Bulfinch. It was almost the last concert of the season, a beautiful program of Telemann and Bach.

James Bolle, the creator and director of Monadnock Music, who lives in Francestown, made a little speech, with his three-year-old daughter clutching him around the knees from behind. John Gibbons, the harpsichordist, played while his tiny daughter in a cherry-colored dress sat on the steps to the platform behind him. After a while sleep overtook her and she lay on the carpeted step, slumbering undisturbed. Other musicians' children were there too, asleep and awake, taking in music through their pores as naturally as the air they breathed.

Monday, September 3

Yesterday in the heat—92 degrees in the afternoon—Elizabeth and I drove to Adams, Massachusetts, where the descendants of Friends hold an annual meeting in the old meetinghouse there. It stands, a gaunt, gray, primitive building, on the summit of a hill, with a wide view of surrounding mountains dominated by Graylock. There is a silent meeting after the manner of Friends for half an hour, then a speaker. Two years ago Elizabeth spoke; this year I did.

In spite of the heat people filled the stiff, narrow, uncomfortable wooden benches. A few were young, a few were men, but most, as always on such occasions, were white-haired women. Six of our friends came from Bennington.

One of them was Marion Smith, Bradford Smith's widow. Brad and Marion had been in Japan before the war, and he had a friendly understanding of the Japanese people. They later had two years in India, and by the time that Violet and I spent two summers in Arlington, Vermont, the Smiths had retired to their lovely old farmhouse in Shaftsbury nearby. We very much enjoyed seeing something of them.

Brad died several years ago, of cancer, looking to his mountains as he grew daily weaker, writing poems and essays of great beauty and serenity. After his death some of his writings were put together and published in a Pendle Hill Pamphlet under the title "Dear Gift of Life." This little book has been of great help to people facing death and to those close to them. With a clear mind and a pure spirit, Bradford Smith combined what seems to me unusual—a great love of life and a complete readiness to depart it when called upon to. He had physical courage in the face of suffering. He died lovingly and completely his own master.

Wednesday, September 5

Driving to Franconia to see Emily Wilson, I went up the fine Highway 93, which bypasses the tawdry tourist spots that used to give the road through the White Mountains the name of "The Flush Toilet Route" in the days when motor courts were primitive. This road soars along the heights through what seems like endless forest. The day was gray and heavy, the clouds low and the air full of moisture. Then the new road ended and we plunged into the narrow road through beautiful Franconia Notch. I could see the Old Man of the Mountain, his face sharp and clear and intellectual, and the immense gold and gray cliffs.

On the other side of the Notch suddenly the air cleared and dried out; the sky turned blue; the distant mountains appeared. When I reached Emily's house on the ridge above the town, it had become a sparkling "mountain day." We sat on her porch, looking straight down the Notch, with Haystack symmetrical on one side, Cannon Mountain enormous and buffalo-like on the other. Now and then a cloud, white and puffy, floated between them. In the foreground her tangled garden was bright with scarlet phlox, and monarch butterflies fluttered about. It was a scene of spectacular beauty.

Emily, who is two years younger than I, is still lame from her fall on the ice last winter. It happened right here in her own driveway, and for a desperate time she lay wondering if she could manage to get herself into the house, knowing that the last person to go past on the road that day, the mailman, had driven by several hours earlier. To lie there in the snow all night would be to freeze to death. It is hard for her to face exchanging her beloved mountains for the Pennsylvania countryside, but this accident has pointed up the wisdom of her decision to sell her house and be a Kendal Founder. And what a lot she has to give to the new community!

We talked and talked.

I started homeward late in the afternoon. Before I reached the Notch a cloud blew across the road, spraying my windshield with moisture. From then on it was dark and gray, damp and heavy, with no distant vision. I had come out of one climate into an entirely different one.

Saturday, September 8. Cold: 56 degrees this morning!

There is much discussion about the title for my book. Friends are prolific with suggestions: "Whittier Speaks to Youth," "Whittier: A Fiery Young Man," "Friend of His Country," "Friend of Mankind," "Whittier: Poet, Politician, Propagandist," and "Who *Is* Whittier?"

But the prize came in a letter: "Dance of Plastic Circumstance." Now what could that mean?

Wednesday, September 12. Harvest moon last night

I have been reading Paul Tournier's *Learn to Grow Old*, which I think is a very pedestrian book, full of well-worn, labored, sound remarks about attitudes of and toward the old. But I did find one or two good things in it.

"What man needs most is not to be alone when he faces death," as if a human presence, even that of an unbeliever, were a pledge of the divine presence. This I am sure is true.

In the old days, when people died at home, there was someone with them. Now they die in hospitals or nursing homes. There are people around, of course, but no nurse has time to sit with a patient hour after hour, waiting. Emily and I talked of the possibility of sitting beside the dying at Kendal, in the times when no one else was there to do it.

184

And Tournier says this about the life after death: "Our minds are totally incapable of conceiving what the other world will be like, of conceiving a world radically different from the present world, as it is presented to our senses, to our experience and to our intellect." This I have been saying myself, for years, ever since, in fact, at fifteen, I saw a locust come up out of the ground, split its hard shell, and emerge with iridescent wings into the sunshine. How could it have imagined what lay ahead?

Birth must be fully as difficult and painful an experience as death. Being thrust out of warmth and safety, forced to struggle through a cramped passage, emerging into a new, cold, foreign atmosphere, forced to use unused lungs by a sudden blow, wrapped in an unfamiliar texture, left alone, alone, alone. And this is normal birth. For some the experience is long-drawn-out; for others there are painful injuries. Di's skull was broken by forceps; the Wilson child had an arm fractured by the doctor's rough handling.

Tournier believes that he will keep his personal identity. I don't, but I don't think I shall miss it. I shall have—I think—intense consciousness, and experience joy and understanding. I want terribly to know, as Piet Hein's Grook has it, "what this whole show is all about."

Wednesday, September 19

A day at the seashore is to a mountain summer as salt to a boiled egg. Elizabeth and I went off with the two Shetland sheep dogs and a picnic basket to the New Hampshire coast. There is only an eighteen-mile stretch of it, but

185

after you get above the horrors of Hampton Beach it is lovely—great wide semicircles of hard, fine sand enclosed by spits of rock, and then the sea and in the distance the Isles of Shoals, where Whittier and Emerson and Sarah Orne Jewett and the rest used to sit on the long hotel porch talking and admiring Celia Thaxter's flowers. The head of a seal was a dark note in the water; there were sailboats, a launch full of sightseers, lobster boats, and a distant freighter making for Portsmouth. Behind us was a narrow strip of road fringed with cottages, and behind them the marshes, blue and golden. Over all soared the great exhilarating vastness of the sky, patterned by small white clouds and the still smaller drifts of birds—herring gulls, black-backed gulls, terns, cliff swallows, sanderlings.

The dogs were ecstatic, fifteen-month-old Nicky seeing the ocean for the first time. She raced over the wide beach, pranced daintily at the water's edge, barked furiously at the boisterous waves that, unlike the water at the pond, rushed at her. Now and then in her joy she pounced on the elderly Gibbie, who turned his back and braced himself for the onslaught.

We ate our lunch sitting on the rocks, and afterward read aloud Camus's lecture, "Create Dangerously," from *Resistance, Rebellion and Death*. There are some wonderful things in it, especially the last sentence:

> Perhaps then, if we listen attentively, we shall hear, amid the uproar of empires and nations, a faint

flutter of wings, the gentle stirring of life and hope. Some will say this hope lies in a nation; others, in a man. I believe rather that it is awakened, revived, nourished by millions of solitary individuals whose deeds and works every day negate frontiers and the crudest implications of history. As a result, there shines forth fleetingly the ever-threatened truth that each and every man, on the foundation of his own sufferings and joys, builds for all.

Home again sunburned and filled to the last pore with ocean air. Jupiter burned in the east and Venus in the west.

Thursday, September 20

As I look forward to Kendal—and I do—I sometimes catch myself thinking of all the nice things I am going to do for those old people there, and then I remember that I am one of those old people myself. I don't think I want anybody doing kindly things for me!

Friday, September 21

Frost this morning was white over the lawn and field and the roofs of house and office and barn. Fortunately I had taken in my fuchsia last night, which, after blooming luxuriantly for three months, still has thirty blossoms on it. When I went out to feed the birds, the grass was stiff and prickly under my feet; the sun was lifting clouds of steam off the roof of the office. First frost in the city passes unno-

187

ticed; here it is an end—and a portent.

At seven the temperature was 30, but at eight it was up to 50. It doesn't last long.

I hung the fuchsia back on its hook on the porch, and a hummingbird came and sat down on a tendril, an enchanting and rather unusual sight. Most of the time hummingbirds are in the air, "pivoting," as that teen-age poet put it, "on nothingness."

But I remember the day in June in the early 1940s when I took a long walk out from Rensselaerville and came on a catalpa tree in full bloom, buzzing oddly. As I drew nearer I saw that it was filled with hummingbirds, evidently a whole migration of them. There must have been at least a hundred, some hovering over the blossoms, others resting on the branches, five or six to a branch, looking like Christmas-tree ornaments.

Saturday, September 22. Rain

I burned the first draft of my Whittier book in the Franklin stove in the office. It takes a long time to burn typewritten pages. I wish I had a shredder of the kind that has been so useful in government offices. Viking has the final typescript (and what do they think of it? They haven't deigned to say), and I have the carbon copy. My files are going to be limited in the future, and I've no intention of bestowing the first draft on a library, to clog up *their* files.

I shall miss this little office where I write. There is nothing in it to distract me: just the stove, some bookshelves, the table and chair, the typewriter stand, and, of course, the view of field and trees and the long humpy line of North and South Pack Monadnock. Bill McGreal used to have his office here and Elizabeth and Nora their weekly story hour for the Peterborough children. There are good "vibes" here.

Sunday, September 23

Busy last day. To Meeting. Then to see the old house which Faith and Joan, our young friends, two copy editors, have bought, having shaken the dust of New York off their editorial heels. Lunch at Elizabeth's with Emily Wilson, who has been spending the night. Laurie Armstrong came to say good-by.

I had "tea" at Nora's on her porch. "Tea" is what we used to call Sunday supper when I was a child. We had dinner—roast beef and ice cream—in the middle of the day, and tea, which, like tea today at Nora's, was tea and salad and hot bread at half past six. When I went to Sunday tea at Catharine Armett's in Edinburgh in 1962, it was a whole table full of things, including sardines and scones. I have always thought that tea in this sense was Scottish, but Nora is English. At any rate, it was nostalgic, and I loved it.

Thursday, September 27

Two days back at Alden Park, I am still noticing the city roar. As I hear it in bed in the early morning, it is a steady low growl, like an animal's, all sounds merged into one. When I take my walk around the edges of Alden Park and

189

especially at the back, where unmowed field meets the Wissahickon woods, I might be miles away from a city, except for the steady roar of traffic, but now the sounds are differentiated into gear shiftings and the separate sounds of trucks and scooting "bugs." Both yesterday and this morning I flushed a pair of pheasants. Asters and eupatoriums are in bloom; the mockingbirds are in full song, and jays are squawking.

The effort of moving and of deciding how to dispose of superfluous possessions looms ahead. What I did last spring was a mere scratching of the surface. I have whole closets stacked with boxes full of precious things.

There is absolutely no way decently to dispose of doctoral hoods, *honoris causa*. Rufus Jones's thirteen doctoral hoods used to be stored on the fifth floor of the stacks of the Haverford College library—I don't know where they are in the new library. No library in the world would be interested in mine. You can't give a hood to anyone, for what possible use is it unless it represents the degree you have, and if you have the degree you have the hood. Opportunities for wearing hoods are extremely limited. No white elephant sale would bother with them, and anyhow, if you did give them away, your ingratitude to the donors would be blatant to the world. You can't throw them away; how shocking on a refuse pile! They are too solid to burn in the fireplace, which is the only facility for burning that I have. Obviously I can't put them into the incinerator with the garbage. You can't cut them up and make anything out of them, even supposing you could bring yourself to be so irreverent. Though perhaps a yard of silk has gone into each lining, the pieces are too oddly shaped and differently colored to make anything but a patchwork quilt. Someone suggested that I send them back to the universities that bestowed them on me. But they aren't marked, and I have forgotten in some cases from which institutions they came. And then the time it would take! Writing letters of explanation, packing up for mailing.

They are like peacocks, stately and colorful with their white velvet trim, their stiff, corded black silk, and their brilliant silk linings—scarlet, scarlet and gray, gold and white, dark blue and silver, light blue and white, blue and brown, green and white—all bright and challenging. When I come right down to it, I don't want to part with my Drexel hood, which was the first one, nor with my North Carolina hood, for that has dear associations, nor my Haverford hood, the first that Haverford ever gave to a woman, nor— So I fold them all up carefully into a large, heavy box and dedicate a shelf of my future storage space to this useless exhibit of prideful display.

Now what about my collection of miniature Japanese toys?

Monday, October 1

A radiantly beautiful October day, just like that one forty years ago. I bought myself some sweetheart roses, as I do on this day. Forty years ago today Morgan was taken from me in a single moment. I can see his smile still as he turned to me from the front seat of the car. All else is lost.

I came back to consciousness in the hospital, my world fallen about my ears.

I have been thinking about the difference in meaning of those two related words, grief and sorrow. Grief, I think, is the first sharp anguish that comes with the realization of loss; sorrow is the long, slow assimilation of grief. Sorrow becomes a companion, a way of life. Grief and joy are at opposite poles, but joy and sorrow often walk hand in hand.

When I reached Japan on October 15, 1946, after two weeks at sea with only the most fragmentary bits of radioed news, one of the first things I learned was that Eastburn Thompson had been killed in an airplane accident on his way to do some work in Europe for the American Friends Service Committee. He was a much-loved member of Germantown Meeting and one of the founders of CARE; I had known him well during the time that both he and I worked for the A.F.S.C. Handsome, idealistic, devoted, he was one of those golden lads who die when they have the world in their hands. My heart ached for his young wife, Nan, who was going through an experience so like my own, except that she was not with her husband when he was killed and she had two small children to bring up alone. It was another one of those inexplicable tragedies. Why, if there is any sense at all in the universe, is such a young life taken while disabled old people wait miserably for release?

Since then Nan has joined the Poets. One day in the

1950s, after I had read some verses of mine on sorrow, she sent me a note enclosing a poem of Robert Nathan's. "Sometimes," she wrote, "does it seem to you almost a blessing to have had sorrow? It or something has brought strength and understanding to me which I know I never had or would have had."

The poem was entitled "Reflections."

> *Love is the first thing,*
> *Love goes past.*
> *Sorrow is the next thing,*
> *Quiet is the last.*

> *Love is a good thing,*
> *Quiet isn't bad,*
> *But sorrow is the best thing*
> *I've ever had.*

She added a postcript: "However—I don't agree—*always!*"

Love, quiet, sorrow: how can anyone say sorrow is better than love? It has taken me many years to understand it. When I wrote of sorrow in *The World in Tune*, I looked at Nathan's poem, but I was not ready to quote it. Now, at seventy-one, I know that sorrow does in its own way bless. Meister Eckhart, writing in the fourteenth century, makes the same strange affirmation: "I say that after God there was never anything that is better than sorrow."

But who would ever stretch out voluntary hands to receive this blessing?

What an advantage the old have—in some ways—over the young! Five weeks ago I sent off the manuscript of my Whittier book, which will be titled *Mr. Whittier*, to The Viking Press. Once I would have been in an agony of suspense until I heard if it was liked, if changes were necessary. Now in these weeks I have given it a passing thought from time to time, quite prepared for it not to be what was wanted, since I am in many ways out of step with the present writing world. Today a letter comes, forwarded from Peterborough, from my editor, saying that I have done a "splendid job" and that I shall be hearing from the copy editor soon. So no major changes are to be made.

I am very much pleased, but—and doubtless this is the other side of the coin—not wildly elated as once I would have been. Still, the letter is a *very* nice birthday present.

Tomorrow I shall be seventy-one.

About the Author

ELIZABETH GRAY VINING was born in Philadelphia shortly after the turn of the century. She was graduated from Bryn Mawr College, and in the years that followed, under the names Elizabeth Janet Gray and Elizabeth Gray Vining, she wrote many books for adults and children, including the Newbery Award winner *Adam of the Road*.

During and immediately after World War II, Mrs. Vining worked for the American Friends Service Committee. In 1946 she was appointed tutor to Crown Prince Akihito of Japan and later wrote the widely read *Windows for the Crown Prince*. She is the author of several novels and biographies, and her autobiography, *Quiet Pilgrimage*, was published in 1970.

Elizabeth Gray Vining lives south of Philadelphia, in Kennet Square, Pennsylvania.